Informing Young Women

To the men in my life:
To my father Leslie, an enlightened MCP.
To my husband Mark, who cooked dinners while I wrote.
To my son Christopher, who has no choice but to become gender-liberated.

Informing Young Women

Gender Equity through Literacy Skills

by LESLEY S. J. FARMER

McFarland & Company, Inc., Publishers
Jefferson, North Carolina, and London

British Library Cataloguing-in-Publication data are available

Library of Congress Cataloguing-in-Publication Data

Farmer, Lesley S. J.
   Informing young women : gender equity through literacy
skills / by Lesley S. J. Farmer.
      p.   cm.
   Includes bibliographical references and index.
   ISBN 0-7864-0240-7 (sewn softcover : 55# alk. paper) ∞
   1. Library orientation for youth.   2. Information retrieval —
Study and teaching — United States.   3. Women — Education —
United States.   I. Title.
Z711.2.F368   1996   96-22468
027.62'6 — dc20   CIP

Manufactured in the United States of America

*McFarland & Company, Inc., Publishers
   Box 611, Jefferson, North Carolina 28640*

Table of Contents

Introduction

Constance Williams, a recent high school graduate when she wrote an article for *School Library Journal*, provides the ultimate reason for this book:

> It has been said that society determines the status of women, while the educational system perpetuates it. Will you help us in the long overdue struggle to break this cycle — and acquire the knowledge we need to eliminate sexism in this society? [p. 36].

Every day the news talks about women and men: the inequalities, the progress, the backlash. Within the business world alone, several trends are noticeable:

• Women's pay has risen significantly over the last two decades. However, on the average, it is still not equal to men's for comparable work.

• More women are CEOs in corporate America than ever before, and more jobs are open to either gender (such as nursing, piloting, construction). The glass ceiling still exists at the top levels, though, for women and other underrepresented groups.

• Affirmative action laws are being removed, and males are suing over reverse discrimination.

On the global level, the 1995 Fourth World Conference on Women highlighted several gender-sensitive issues:

• Women comprise three-quarters of the poor in the United States.

• Only six women head national governments.

• Two-thirds of illiterates worldwide are women, and they are educated at a slower rate than men.

• In the United States, a woman is battered every eighteen minutes.

It is within this environment that today's children are being educated. Here are some of the realities recently noted by the Women's Action Coalition and analyst Daniel Evan Weiss:

• Worldwide, there are 80 million more boys than girls in primary and secondary school.

• In elementary and junior high school classes, boys are eight times more likely to call out for attention than girls.

• In classrooms of coed colleges, female students speak 2½ times less often than male students.

1

• Two percent of school superintendents are female; 98 percent of kindergarten teachers are female.

Where do these discrepancies come from? And how can they be confronted and changed? How do gender issues affect students? Do curricula deal with gender? What attitudes about gender are reflected in teaching practices and the school community? Especially as these youth must deal with societal issues, and can make decisions that affect how people of either gender are treated, education is a keystone for making a difference in today's children and tomorrow's world.

As adolescents, students become increasingly aware of gender issues. They are coping with their own physical changes, much of which are gender-linked. They are more aware of gender-based relationships. They are more cognizant of mass media signals about gender. And they are increasingly conscious of the political and societal realities around them.

One educational skill stands out in this quest for gender understanding and equity: information literacy. In this information age, access to and manipulation of information is a valuable set of skills for young people, for it enables them to examine social messages and assumptions rather than feel manipulated by them. By determining what they need to know, by finding the sources of information, by selecting the information they need, by making it meaningful for them in their own settings, and by sharing that information with others to provide mutual support, students discover the realities of gender issues and can act on them.

Thus, this book is geared to helping librarians and other educators in general to empower young women *and men* through information and information skills. Gender issues are a focal point because content and content delivery have historically minimized women's contributions and perspectives, and students can have the opportunity to resolve these issues. In addition, educators can foster a gender-inclusive learning environment.

The first chapter points out the gender issues that exist in many educational settings, and provides a historical and social context that demonstrates the need for examining them.

The second chapter looks at self-esteem issues, and provides ways for teachers to introduce activities that foster critical self-examination so students can gather information about themselves and use that data to improve their self-concepts.

The third chapter examines gender-associated ways of learning. It looks at biological and social issues that can enrich students' learning experiences.

The fourth chapter offers an organizational structure that accommodates a variety of perspectives for learning. It emphasizes an inclusive learning community, and deals with the varied levels of implementing gender awareness and inclusiveness.

The fifth chapter looks at the specific issue of information literacy: how students interact with information to solve problems. It also points out how focusing on gender issues helps develop a more complex and richer research context.

The sixth chapter reviews how to plan and implement learning activities that foster gender equity and a sense of inclusiveness. It challenges classroom and librarian teachers to examine their course content and the resources they use. Emphasis is placed on teacher-librarian partnerships, which models a collaborative spirit.

The seventh chapter provides a framework for developing reality-based lesson plans that incorporate gender issues. A series of ready-made lessons follows to provide guidelines for meaningful learning and action.

A subject-arranged bibliography of significant resources that deal with gender issues is located at the end of the book.

Women's liberation was a catchphrase two decades ago. Since then society has become more aware that all humanity needs respect and power. By focusing on gender issues, educators and students can broaden their concepts of education and the means to facilitate positive social change. This notion is a very idealistic one, but we educators are the designated dreamers of society and the shapers of tomorrow. We need to acknowledge our own potential power — and use it to stop the cycle of inequality.

Chapter 1

Why Study Gender Issues?

The most exciting thing about women's liberation is that this century will be able to take advantage of talent and potential genius that have been wasted because of taboos.
— Helen Reddy

THE HEART OF THE MATTER

Are men and women really different? Aren't we the same species? Shouldn't we treat everyone the same? Aren't gender issues really a throwback to sexism? These questions reflect the feeling of many people who believe that equality is here. In a way, it's like being gender-blind. Let's look at the validity of such attitudes.

Women constitute half of the world's population, but they do not represent half of educational content or attention. This inequality is making the headlines these days as studies, such as the American Association of University Women's report, reveal that girls are not getting the same quality of education as are boys. Teachers, both male and female, tend to pay more attention to boys and give them more feedback. Learning strategies also favor male patterns; one study about SAT scores showed that when girls were given more time to answer the questions they improved — while boys didn't.

Female students lack power if they do not gain confidence using some learning tools to the degree that boys do. Particularly as they enter middle school and beyond, computer use by girls drops. Interest in math and science drops. And teachers may expect less from girls in these areas, rather than giving them an extra boost and encouragement. Even though girls often receive higher grades than boys do in the same high school classes, sometimes they self-select not to take more challenging courses out of fear of failure (Sanders).

In fact, pre- and early adolescence marks a critical turning point in girls' education. The socialization process of maturation tends to accentuate

5

gender differences, to the detriment of young women. Girls struggle to find and follow the new rules of conduct, and their formal education suffers, especially when they seem to get more immediate approval for care-taking than for risk-taking (Pipher).

Probably the main gender inequity in education, though, exists in terms of content. Females still do not find themselves in their textbooks to the extent that males do. With fewer role models to identify with, females do not gain self-confidence as easily as do their male counterparts. Girls do not see many women in roles of power and control, so they may feel less powerful themselves. (The 1993 U.N. survey on women's status notes that only six women head governments.) Nor do the values often associated with femininity, such as nurturing and intuition, enjoy equal educational status as problem-solving and debate (Schaef).

The saddest part of this situation is that it diminishes education and empowerment for both sexes. Inequities result in lower self-esteem, rendering students less capable of realizing their full potential and contributing to society. Students do not experience as many ways of learning or glean from everyone's wisdom to the degree that they could, so they do not have a full repertoire with which to work. Since the wisdom of women has been overlooked or underrated for centuries, students are kept from vital information from older role models as well as from their female contemporaries.

By addressing and resolving gender issues in education, both females and males become empowered to learn and share their insights — and respect their differences. This book examines one way to foster gender equity: through information skills.

TESTING THE WATERS

What are some of the myths and realities about gender issues, particularly as they apply to education? How aware are you about today's young women? This short quiz may provide new insights.

True or False

1. By kindergarten most children are aware of most forms of bias, including race and gender bias.   *true*

2. Girls' self-esteem drops significantly when they enter early adolescence.   *true*

3. Older girls and women more often link their successes with luck and their failures to their own limitations, while boys and men link success to their own efforts and failure to others' responsibilities.   *true*

4. Teachers call on boys 80 percent more often than they call on girls. *true*

5. Historians link girls' lack of self-esteem to the fact that few K–12 courses mention women's achievements. *true*

6. Fifteen percent of college physics or engineering majors are women. *true*

7. In coed colleges, female students speak in class 2½ times less often than male students. *true*

8. Girls have a 40 percent chance of heading a family with children. *true*

9. Women are projected to account for nearly 60 percent of labor force entrants between 1990 and 2005. *true*

10. College-educated Hispanic women earn less than white male high school graduates. *true*

(Facts drawn from Sadker, Weiss, Women's Action Coalition.)

HOW DID THIS INEQUITY HAPPEN?

The intricate ties between biology and society have existed from pre-history. However, the manifestations of these ties have differed over time. Shari Thurer's fascinating book *The Myths of Motherhood* traces the close correlation between respect towards women and the status of motherhood. Thurer asserts that the neolithic era may have been the golden age for mothers, because both sexes had valuable roles and equal status and power. Nature and people were one. With the advent of city life apart from nature and its corollary partitioning of the public and private realms, patriarchies sprang up and women's roles were reduced, Thurer asserts.

Certainly, women's roles and status have changed throughout history. In some cultures, those roles may be more prescribed. In other cultures, females' options are much broader — and may be more confusing. These roles have their basis in several factors:

- Biology: e.g., women bear children.
- Religion: e.g., women cannot become Catholic priests.
- Economics: e.g., men tend to do more heavy manual labor.
- Social/cultural expectations: e.g., the display of thighs is taboo for Tongan women.
- Politics: e.g., some women have not been considered citizens or have not been able to vote.
- Education: e.g., some courses, such as carpentry or sewing, have been single-sex.
- Law: e.g., abortions are illegal in Ireland.

The fundamental issue, though, is that gender is a social phenomenon, not a strictly biological footnote.

In contemporary society, each girl re-enacts that biological and social interplay. At birth, girls and boys display an innocent wholeness. Their bodies, minds, and emotions are well aligned; for instance, physical discomfort brings forth cries of frustration. While genders may differentiate their preferences for toys or actions to some extent, *in their own minds* boys and girls do not consider their choices as being inherently better because of gender; they consider difference a neutral value.

In helping children learn to differenti*ate*, society may layer judgment with a moral and status differenti*al*. By school age, boys have been known to say that dolls are inferior because girls like them, *and girls are inferior* or at least not as important as boys. What about dolls that boys like? Those toys are typically masculinized with the help of manufacturing "accomplices" to assume the forms of monsters, robots, militia and other "male-approved" images. Despite stereotypes, little girls get into just as much trouble as do boys, and they get just as violent. However, adults are less comfortable with these "roughhouse" girls. Adults are probably trying to help young people adjust to the behavior social norms expected upon maturation. Nevertheless, adult disapproval sometimes seems to reflect adults' needs to reinforce differences as much as it aids the self-identification of their offspring. Most children get the social messages quickly and start to section off their identities in order to keep important adult approval. Girls may begin to think one thing and say or do another. Still, prepubescent children tend to achieve about the same in school and have about the same level of self-esteem (Pipher).

The physical and emotional changes experienced in adolescence, though, brush away any remnants of wholeness/undifferentiation and psychological innocence. For both boys and girls, bodies and emotions may feel like alien entities to their self-identities; they cannot fully control either of them. Boys, however, are heralded for their grown-up ways; girls are more likely to be shamed. Menarche is the most obvious source of discomfort. Even now, few women will discuss those embarrassing moments. Men may feel that they will suffer if they can't satisfy their sexual frustration, but girls face a lifetime commitment of motherhood if they consummate their sexual fantasies. And males are more tolerated for their behavior than females are.

The psychological changes in adolescent females is even more devastating, though, because they are subtler. The social rules of boys and girls differ, if for no other reason than that adolescence signals the rules are "for keeps." Even first graders these days talk about "sexing" and pairing. For teens, though, Barbies and Kens are replaced by real bodies and real babies. Societal pressures are real too: to be liked, to be cute, to be feminine. In junior high school when the rational brain is more likely to be "on hold" according to Piaget, socialization skills are paramount. During this stage, girls have a more difficult time than boys do in learning new ways to behave and think because girls have to change their behaviors more. Boys can still be boys, but girls are encouraged to stop their assertiveness. Girls "suddenly" act dumber, especially in stereotypically male-linked subjects such as mathematics and the hard sciences. Girls have become aware of the imbalance in power between the sexes (Mann, p. 177).

How do young teenage girls react? Pipher offers a number of typical responses: in submission, in rebellion, in pain, and sometimes in self-affirmation. In the first instance, they deny their self-identities and react passively to their environment in an effort to gain approval. They go along with the game, from dressing according to standard expectations to getting the right boyfriend and taking the less-academically challenging courses. They may become withdrawn or mentally lost. In the second case, girls fight by opposition and sometimes self-destruct. They may dress provocatively or very "masculinely." They may become overly aggressive and rebellious. In other words, they may exaggerate their behaviors and end up alienated, pregnant, or permanently mentally scarred. In the third option, girls find ways to express their frustration: in writing, in eating disorders, in self-mutilation, in artistic description, in exercise, in hobbies. With self-affirmation they work through their pain and frustration to develop coping skills that help them gain more power and self-assurance.

EXISTING EDUCATIONAL METHODS TO ADDRESS INEQUITIES

The question may arise: aren't the schools addressing this issue? What about equal opportunity? What about sex education? What about girls' sports?

These are all valid steps that schools can and do take. But they aren't enough in themselves. Dealing with gender inequities involves every part of the educational system. Gender issues do not exist only outside the school community; they are integral to it. And that attitude must be infused throughout the curriculum and every other component of the education process from the principal to the janitor, from the textbook to co-curricular activities.

Typically, schools do not consciously try to undermine the self-esteem of young women. Rather, their actions betray a lack of awareness of their covert messages. Sometimes, by failing to acknowledge subtle gender differences, they negate the very real diversity of their students. Seldom are teachers videotaped to record how their verbal and body language distinguishes between the sexes. Seldom are curriculum decisions made on the basis of gender needs or abilities. Seldom do schools question the very assumptions of education and its delivery as it relates to gender issues.

WHAT GENDER-EQUITY EDUCATION ENTAILS

Particularly since schools are in the business of learning, they have a responsibility to learn about gender issues. The central issue is really not women, per se; it's about pluralism: how different perspectives can be respected, accepted, embraced. The first stage is consciousness about inclusion and exclusion. Does the curriculum include the perspectives of women and other underrepresented groups? Does it acknowledge the contributions of these peoples? Does the curriculum content note the conditions and circumstances of women across classes and cultures? Does the curriculum approach learning in a cross-disciplinary way so more transference of learning can occur?

The next aspect of gender deals with interpretations of information. Do students and staff recognize the social context of data? No one is objective; each person brings her/his biases and values to the content she/he is investigating. Are social norms and assumptions tested? All learning is contextual — or relational — embedded; students need to test the social assumptions of information given to them. Students should differentiate between abstract and relational thinking, and know how to engage in both types of processing. They should construct meaningful realities from multiple perspectives.

Finally, gender issues influence teaching and learning methodologies. Does the teacher facilitate learning, providing a supportive climate rather than dictating the right way to learn? Do students have a chance to work collaboratively and independently? Is process as important as product? Does learning transfer to real world and relational skills? In the final analysis, is learning real?

Feminist scholarship and gender-equitable practice broaden the scope of traditional education and equip young people with the skills they need to succeed as humane persons in a widely diverse and changing environment.

HOPEFUL TRENDS

But what of tomorrow? Ideally, all peoples should be empowered in a healthy world. While society continues to be in a state of flux, several realities have permeated the American mind that could bode well for female imperatives. *Megatrends for Women* offers several encouraging signs:

Environmental issues have gained international attention; the concept of "gaia," the living earth, affirms the need for interdependence with one another and with nature. Women understand this symbiotic relationship, and can take a leading role in furthering such causes.

Family issues raise the point about the importance of the first years of life and the need for society to support parental efforts. Day care and health coverage are two legislative indicators that families and child-rearing matter.

Economic issues underline the growing need for two-income families, and industry accommodation for family and personal needs. As women have gained a foothold in the door of economic opportunity, they are beginning to see that they can bring their own leadership styles to the board table and be taken seriously.

Leisure issues emphasize the need for exercise and recreational socialization for both sexes. Studies show that self-esteem for both sexes increases with participation in sports. Title IX marked the beginning of federal support for women's athletics, and more women are engaging in sports for fun and profit.

Ethical and spiritual issues are more in the forefront. Professional schools are incorporating ethics into their curriculums, and people are increasingly demanding about moral values in the public arena. The general public sees women as more capable of keeping values in mind, partly because of women's traditional roles and partly because women haven't been included for as long in the seemingly corruptible corporate or political rings. Religion is experiencing a rebirth with goddess worship and nature spirituality, with a critical eye toward patriarchical organizations.

Information issues point out the need for brain over brawn. Equitable access to information and ethical manipulation of those sources can empower women and give them the needed tools to succeed in tomorrow's world.

Particularly for a society in transition as it examines gender issues, the time is ripe to provide students with the information skills they need to learn about their society and how to make it work for them. As young people become more aware of gender issues, they can broaden their knowledge base and human perspective. They can become more human and more humane. Today's teachers can have a decided effect on youth by providing them with opportunities to build on these contemporary trends, with an eye to gender consciousness, so that youth can empower themselves — and each other — and can make a difference in their future world.

Chapter 2

Getting Personal: Raising Self-Esteem

Though we travel the world over to find the beautiful, we must carry it with us or we will find it not.
— Ralph Waldo Emerson

WHY GET PERSONAL?

Teaching information skills generates gender equity, while a learning community is the environment touted for effective learning. Underlying this process, though, is the need for direct attention to student self-esteem. As a recent California Department of Education study confirmed, in students without a positive self-concept and the grounds for respectful and trusting relationships, complex skills will go unheeded or underutilized. These findings confirm Maslov's earlier theory that the basic human needs for safety and security must be satisfied before self-realization can be thoughtfully explored.

The issue of self-esteem is particularly sensitive for teenage girls. Repeated studies (American Association of University Women, Eagle, Gilligan, Mikel-Brown, Orenstein, Pipher, Sadker) document the significant drop in self-esteem experienced by girls as they enter puberty. Their self-identify is at risk as they seek to find a niche in a suddenly changing world. Before a self-destructive cycle of frustration and disappointment spins out of control, educators can intervene and help young women regain their self-confidence.

Indeed, self-esteem often depends on self-knowledge. Having an accurate picture of oneself makes accepting and improving oneself easier. Thus, acquiring information skills and improving self-esteem can be interdependent. Indeed, gathering information about one's self is a natural way to acquire information skills. Babies do it the moment they are born. Sometimes teens forget this important lesson as they look outward to the kinds of people they want to imitate. The social messages given to girls, in particular, reinforce that need to adapt to other people's expectations rather than rely on one's own beliefs and values. Examining one's self thoughtfully provides a powerful emotional context for learning, and the information skills picked up in this process will be transferred to other contexts.

This chapter provides some tips for teachers to help students use information skills in exploring their identities and grounding themselves in a healthy and realistic self-assessment and self-acceptance. Concurrently, students can compare their assessments with others as a way to make connections, particularly in terms of gender issues.

NOTES TO EDUCATORS

On a subconscious level, at least, students deal with self-esteem issues every day. How they react to teachers and students, how they act around their families, how they handle real world pressures: those attitudes and behaviors reflect how young people feel about themselves. So it makes sense to incorporate self-esteem activities throughout the curriculum rather than to relegate such reflection to a lesson within health education or a chapter in a psychology class.

Digging into oneself is a very vulnerable act; thus, mutual trust and respect between teacher and student must be in place before in-depth self-searching is conducted. If a long-term effort is being made to examine self-esteem, educators would do well to start with less personally threatening activities before advancing into soul-searching, sensitive issues. Moreover, some students may feel very uncomfortable about sharing their findings. Reflective writing is a safe way to help those students externalize their feelings and findings without fear of exposure. Students should also have the option to "pass" during class discussions about personal matters. In all cases, integrity and confidentiality must be maintained.

In the final analysis, self-esteem really is lived out on a one-to-one basis as people negotiate personal relationships. While it is necessary for teachers to establish safe and open atmospheres for learning, they must also build individual trusting relationships with each and every student. This can be a daunting task, especially for school librarians who may see a particular student only occasionally throughout the year! So what are some ways to make that happen? Berne and Savary's book on building self-esteem in children offers some practical advice.

• Be available. This shows that you care enough about youth to be around them.

• Listen nonjudgmentally. This shows you respect youth's feelings and thoughts.

• Remember their names, the most glorious sound in most people's ears. Use their names when speaking with them.

• Share with them. This shows that you value the relationship enough to share part of yourself.

• Emphasize similarities, so youth won't think they're alone.

• Come prepared. This shows students that they are worth thinking about ahead of time.

• Be authentic. This encourages youth to be real with you.

• Be nonthreatening through careful wording and body language. This sets the tone for mutual respect and lessens self-doubt.

• Build success into the relationship. This encourages youth to feel comfortable and competent with adults.

• Provide opportunities for students to choose. This helps them become more responsible, more self-motivated, and more in control of their lives.

• Acknowledge and accept emotions. This validates a young person's feelings and fosters self-acceptance.

• Use humor. Laughter can provide a safe outlet in sometimes tense times.

• Expect students to test your care. Students need to find the limits of acceptance. They also need to know that you care about them, even when you dislike their actions. Young people are the most trying when they are trying to find the trust they need in order to raise their self-esteem.

WHO AM I?

"Who do you think you are?" Until students seriously ask themselves that question, they will have a difficult time analyzing their relationships with the world around them. They need to be well-informed about themselves so they can establish a strong foundation for meaningful learning.

• Have students list five things they really value or admire, and five things they really despise. Have them look for possible patterns within or between lists. This exercise helps them discover their motivations.

• Persons often learn more from their failures than their successes. Have students think of a time when they failed or had trouble doing something. How did they respond to the problem? What did they learn? How can they use that knowledge in dealing with the future?

• Families and cultural heritage help to shape personalities. Have students list family and cultural values and traditions. Have them compare those values with a partner.

• The extended family includes those relatives, friends, and other significant people who support and guide a person. Have each student draw a circle in the middle of a page, and write her/his own name inside it. Have them draw other circles around the central one, labeling each with the name of a significant extended family member. Draw a line from each circle to the central one, and label each line with a word describing that person's influence in the student's life. Have students compare these family webs.

• Each person has unique qualities and experiences. Have students pretend to be biographers of their own lives so they can discover their central uniqueness. Have students write about themselves in the third person, describing themselves at one point in early elementary school, in the present at a social gathering with peers, in the future at their ideal peak, and near the end of their lives. They should include details: settings, associated people, actions, feelings. What do these life scripts say about student values and self-perceptions?

THE PRIVATE ME AND THE PUBLIC ME

How people feel about themselves may differ from how they think others feel about them. Here are some exercises to examine those differences and similarities.

• Have students fill in a Personal Strength Square:

Four traits you like in yourself:	Four things your friends like about you:
Four accomplishments you are proud of:	Four things you can do that you feel good about:

Students can share these squares with a partner, or have pairs complete a square about each other. Students can transform their squares into coats of armor by drawing one image from each quadrant onto their personal "shield." This exercise helps students recognize their strengths and learn how past accomplishments increase future success rate.

• Another way to examine the differences between the private person and the public person is to categorize perceptions into four "cells":

OTHERS: SELF:	THE KNOWN	THE UNKNOWN
THE KNOWN	We both know something about me.	Others don't know something I know about myself.
THE UNKNOWN	Others know something about me that I don't know.	Neither of us knows something about me.

In pairs, have students fill out the grid, and compare their findings. Note particularly where perceptions differ; have students reflect on the reasons for the discrepancies. This exercise can be expanded to compare perceptions in different role settings: family, school, and social.

• Students play out different roles in their lives as they relate to themselves and others. These roles can be categorized according to school life, family life, community life, personal life. Have them list all the roles they play, such as: daughter, friend, soccer player, Candy Striper, Buddhist, Mexican, worrier. Have them rank their relative importance to themselves, then to others (e.g., parents, teachers, friend). Have them analyze their findings.

• Persons usually show only parts of themselves to the public. Have students make public masks, and have them explain their significance. They may wear a different "mask" in different situations or with different people. Have students share those differences and the reasons for their masks.

• Usually persons understand one another when their backgrounds are similar. Have students list three people with whom they can talk easily; have them write down why it is easy to communicate with them. Next, have students list three people with whom they have difficulty talking; have them write down why it is hard to communicate with them. Then have students review their lists and discover any patterns. Have students discuss how can they use that knowledge to improve their communication skills.

HOW CAN I BECOME MY BEST SELF?

Once students have an accurate picture of who they are, and where they are, then they can begin to make plans about where they want to go in life and how they want to grow. These exercises look at dreams and their possible realities.

• In the midst of good times, persons tend to feel better and act more positively. Have students describe their good times. What makes them feel good about those experiences? Do these times tend to focus on one area of life or one group of associates? What personal traits or actions can be strengthened to extend those good times?

• Have students quickly complete this sentence ten times (with no repetitions): I wish _____. Have them analyze their wishes: what patterns emerge, what obstacles emerge, what changes can be made.

• Have students interview someone whom they feel has a good self-concept. Have them determine how that person developed high self-esteem.

• Have each student draw a circle, dividing it into six pie pieces. Label one piece "school," another "friends," another "exercise," another "romance/adventure," another "free time," and the other "spirituality." Next, have each student place a dot in each piece to show to what extent that feel s/he feels satisfied in that area of her/his life. By connecting the dots, students can see the balance, or lack of it, in their lives.

• "A goal is a dream with a plan." Have students visualize what they want to accomplish. Then have them develop a plan of goals, both academic and personal. Each goal should include a specific outcome by a specific date, such as: "I will make the varsity swim team by next February." Each plan should include specific steps to be accomplished by a specific date, such as: "I will do 20 backstroke laps three times a week." Goals may require a change in attitudes or actions, so the plan should identify possible conflicts and ways to overcome them, such as: "I'will need to go to bed earlier and get up earlier so I can practice swimming in the morning." In addition, the plan should include a means of accountability, such as: "My swimming coach will test me each week." Have students make a one-month, one-semester, and one-year action plan.

• Have students try this CRAFTy tip to help them improve their self-esteem:

Cancel false negative self-images. Stop listening to negative inner voices.

Replace negative images with successful, realistic images. Get into the habit of feeling good.

Affirm your self-image to yourself and others.

Focus on goals and immediate strategies to achieve short-term objectives.

Train yourself in new, successful roles. (Farmer, 1995, p. 34)

Chapter 3

Inclusive Ways
of Learning

I'm just a person trapped inside a woman's body. — Elaine Boosler

Whether women are better than men I cannot say — I can say they are certainly no worse. — Golda Meir

IN THE BEGINNING

Where does biology stop and social conditioning start? Some say at age three, others say at birth, others say it's in the genes. Around six weeks after gestation, sexual identity begins to be formed. Studies show that testosterone injections in pregnant laboratory animals have created female offspring that are more aggressive than non-injected females. Baby girls make more babbling and cooing sounds than baby boys, which parents reinforce; this interaction helps females get a head start in developing verbal skills (Hotchkiss, p. 41). As infants, the sexes differ in the ways they play. Regardless of the time frame, by the time that a child enters school, sexual differences in learning exist (Moir).

More importantly, the school as a learning environment exhibits gender-linked characteristics. Textbooks feature male figures more than females, up to six times as often, and characterizations are frequently stereotypical (Sanford, p. 181). Schools that encourage student participation reinforce boys' attention-getting behaviors while encouraging girls to be quiet (Mann, p. 85). Schools often reinforce logical reasoning, a trait typically stronger in males, and downplay emotional and intuitive learning, abilities that girls are more likely to have (Moir, p. 48). As early as first grade, parents' expectations for their daughters' abilities in mathematics are lower than for their sons' (Mann, p. 99). Sometimes the educational card deck seems stacked.

This chapter provides different ways of looking at learning and emphasizes the need for a broad range of teaching and learning techniques that give students a rich repertoire for empowered action. Ultimately, women will not be measured against men; rather, they will be measured individually against themselves — just as men should be measured. No one way is superior, just different.

THE MYTHICAL QUEST

Just as heroes undergo a personal quest to become their best selves, so too do women experience a lifelong journey to become heroines. Murdock looks at this female search as a personal quest, Noble takes a societal perspective, and Estes uses an archetypal approach. In each case, though, a major difference exists between male and female searches for self-identity; for women, the concept of "relationships" is a key focus. As with males, the female quest is fraught with danger and the unknown; unchosen circumstances are encountered and must be dealt with. Psychologically, some of these shadows represent the "dark" or "wild" side of women, the subconscious or suppressed desires that society does not condone. Those encounters require decision-making; the process of choosing is as important as the situation itself. During the quest, old relationships must be examined; in some cases they must be shunted off, in other cases they must be resolved and strengthened. New relationships must be risked and embraced. Women tend to vacillate between male and female figures during their quest; in the final analysis, they must make peace with both sexes and incorporate the best features of each within their psyches.

HOW WOMEN VIEW THEMSELVES

While young girls generally see themselves as competent, maturing women tend to underestimate themselves and their power. Young adolescent women, in particular, lose self-esteem as they try to relate to their peers and their changing bodies (Orenstein, Pipher). Sensitive to social messages, young women begin to feel inferior to men. Girls tend to pay more attention to their appearance than do boys, not only because of physical changes but because they feel that they are being judged socially on their looks more than their male counterparts (Eagle, p. 157). Uncomfortable with their bodies and their maturing emotions, growing girls have a difficult time resolving their sexual natures. Too often, women feel outclassed and alienated in the patriarchal society, somehow feeling that they cannot catch up or be regarded with the same power as men (Mann). While individual women have achieved great success or feel fully self-realized, too many women quietly lead unfulfilled lives (French).

PHYSIOLOGICAL COMPONENTS OF LEARNING

Along the way, differences between the genders has been explained in terms of biology. During a brief period of the twentieth century all discrepancies were credited to socialization; men and women were inherently the same. However, the last several years have seen a resurgence of claims based on biologically-determined factors. (This author personally prefers a social basis for difference, for then each person has a chance for self-determination and change. In fact, a basic tenet in this book is that educators can help young people, and girls in particular, to construct their own lives.)

The current trends in thinking about gender-linked learning patterns, synthesized well in Moir's and Jessel's book, are outlined below. It should be noted that differences are only patterns and not truisms for all people. In any social group, the saddest corollary of gender-based differentiation is lowered self-esteem when a person of either gender doubts her/his own identity and sexual normalcy because s/he doesn't fit the prescribed roles or expectations.

Stimulus and response: Men tend to respond more readily to things rather than people, as opposed to women. Male's spatial ability is greater. They tend to be more aggressive and competitive. Female eyes are more sensitive to the longwave spectrum of light, and they have more directional-sensitive hearing. They also develop speech-related skills earlier. As a result, women tend to be more context-oriented than men and thus less rule-constrained (Moir, p. 18).

Brain patterns: The brain is organized according to gender-linked hormones; behaviors and personal preferences begin at birth, are accentuated at puberty, and regress to the norm with age. Male brains seem to be more abstract; female brains tend to accentuate detail and relationships. Female brain functions are more widely distributed so they can adapt more easily.

The brain can also be examined in terms of its three parts: the R-complex or reptilian brain, the limbic system, and the neocortex. The reptilian brain can be considered the Id partner; the oldest part of the brain, it serves as the body maintenance center. The limbic system acts as the superego buffer zone between the two other parts, and also controls the emotional system. The neocortex is the creative and abstract ego; it plans and forecasts. All parts of the brain need to be addressed in education; women, with their emphasis on relationships, tend to acknowledge this reality more than men do — and more than the traditional educational system does (Caine, p. 59).

Development: Girls tend to enter puberty earlier than do boys. In addition, the order of primary and secondary changes differ between the sexes. For example, while girls' growth spurts usually predate boys', boys' genitals reach maturity some time before girls' counterparts do. These differences can affect academic and social progress, especially as emotional reactions affect ongoing academics. Relative to gender differences:

> Early maturing males tend to experience greater social approval and recognition than their late maturing counterparts. Conversely, early maturing females may have a more difficult time adjusting to pubertal changes than their late maturing peers [Center for Early Adolescence, p. 213].

While it may seem counter-productive to point out sexual differences since women want to be treated equally, females do themselves a disservice by disregarding their very real physical conditions. For example, an uncomfortable menstrual period can affect test-taking behavior, yet how many women will ask for a re-test? A healthier attitude may be to accept differences and find ways for each person, regardless of gender, to reach full potential.

The greatest insight about physiological effects on learning is the recognition that a variety of elements influence the ways in which people process stimuli. *Environment* can make a difference because people react differently to sound, light, temperature, and the space around them. *Physical* conditions of each person differ in terms of sight and other senses, mobility, and health conditions (e.g., illnesses and malnutrition).

The most effective way for educators to approach physiological differences in learning is to promote awareness, acceptance and inclusiveness for all students. Students with different strengths should have the opportunity to act as coaches for others who are less gifted in those areas of expertise. Teachers can set up simulations so students can experience what it might feel like to be blind.

DIFFERENT KINDS OF INTELLIGENCES

Professionals are becoming more aware of the multiple aspects of intelligence. While the battle still rages as to the relative power of heredity and environment to determine these abilities, and the relative degree of sex-linked traits, educators have the ability to encourage all of these skills. In fact, a basic approach to learning should be to engage all of the intelligences so students can use their strengths and can also improve their weaker modes. The following descriptions provide a gender-sensitive construct (Armstrong, Moir).

Word smart (linguistic): Women tend to talk in order to develop relationships, while men tend to give objective information. Women tend to be more linguistically sensitive, conscious of verbal nuances.

Picture smart (spatial): Men tend to be more adept at spatial relationships.

Music smart (musical): Both men and women exhibit musical talent.

Body smart (kinesthetic): Girls tend to focus on detail, while boys concentrate on gross motor skills.

Logic smart (mathematical and scientific): Males tend to dominate females in this arena.

People smart (social sense): Women tend to be more sensitive to non-verbal clues and are able to make connections with people.

Self smart (intrapersonal): Women tend to be more in tune with themselves emotionally; men tend to take a more clinical approach to self-analysis.

As these different intelligences are recognized, teachers need to embed them across the curriculum, and incorporate them in their assessments. In terms of basic teaching methodology, however, educators and students need to practice all intelligences. Here are some strategies that teachers can use to address these different learning styles when designing learning experiences and assessments:

Word smart: These students think in words and love reading and writing. Teachers can give lectures and written assignments.

Picture smart: These students learn through images. Teachers can *show* knowledge through videos, visuals, games, and graphs.

Music smart: These students learn through rhythms and melodies and by listening. Teachers can use songs, raps, instruments, "superlearning," and body rhythms.

Body smart: These students learn through hands-on experiences such as drama, sports, dance, manipulatives, and other sensations. Teachers can use games, equipment, drama, movement, and other tactile experiences.

Logic smart: These students use reason to learn. Teachers can provide experiments, puzzles, and calculators.

People smart: These students bounce ideas off people. Teachers can offer cooperative learning activities, peer coaching, simulations, games, and clubs.

Self smart: These students reflect on their inner workings. Teachers can suggest goal-setting, journals, meditation, and self-paced projects.

OTHER COGNITIVE COMPONENTS OF LEARNING

Messick defines cognitive style as the way that a person perceives, remembers, thinks and solves problems. Several factors besides mode of intelligence are factors under this umbrella of learning.

Conceptual tempo refers to the timing mechanism of the brain. Girls tend to approach a problem cautiously, using a reflective approach. Boys are more apt to think impulsively. This latter approach characterizes risk-takers and curiosity-driven students. While children usually become more reflective with age, school tends to pay more attention to the impulsive learners.

Teachers need to give reflective learners adequate time to think through their answers, and provide opportunities for them to practice behaviors before a test-taking or high risk-taking activity occurs. For impulsive learners, teachers need to structure time and learning steps to channel energy. They should incorporate kinesthetic activities to provide immediate feedback, but also reward students for delayed behavior.

Psychological differentiation deals with field dependence-independence. The field independent learner is able to abstract stimuli and isolate it, a trait more often seen in males. The field dependent learner, more typically female, takes context into consideration when making a critical judgment. Traditional education favors the field-independent learner. However, cooperative learning favors the field-dependent learner (Reiff, p. 9).

Mindstyles is a construct (Reiff, p. 16), that maintains that people use either abstract or concrete thinking, and that they organize information either sequentially or randomly. Most people favor one or two combinations of learning styles: concrete sequential (sequential hands-on learning), concrete random (trial-and-error), abstract sequential (decoding), or abstract random (holistic and emotional reflection, the most likely style used by girls). Teachers should provide opportunities for matched styles and also mismatching so students can broaden their repertoires for learning.

AFFECTIVE COMPONENTS OF LEARNING

Probably the key word in women's approach to learning is "relationships." Whether it is to self, peers, or to ideas, the underlying idea of knowledge is to connect the known with the unknown through the affective domain. This basic assumption underlies all of the following manifestations of women's ways of learning (Belenky):

Collaboration/cooperation: Women work together to develop meaningful knowledge. They derive strength from each other's experiences and insights.

Holistic: Women accept the interdependence between mind and body. They realize that true learning involves internalization and a call to action in the real world.

Interpersonal: Women make connections about learning with other people. They realize that information is socially embedded, and they construct a more accurate picture about a situation by looking at the relations between ideas and humanity.

Connections with feelings: Women realize that authentic knowledge cannot exist independent of emotions. Every idea contains an emotional perspective.

Multidimensional thought: Women construct meaning through multi-dimensional intellectual investigation. Mainstream thought as well as individual achievement must be investigated to develop a well-rounded perspective.

Conformity and dependency: Women tend to be more conformist and interdependent.

Decision-making as clarified consensus: Women often strive towards consensus as they make decisions. Their emphasis is on understanding each person's perspective, and promoting a win-win situation that recognizes individual needs as well as institutional requirements.

Process vs. product: Women tend to acknowledge the validity of process more than men. Product, according to feminist methodology, should arise from process and not undermine it.

Dynamic/changing knowledge: Women accept the evolving nature of knowledge more readily than men do. Women see information as a gradual gathering and sifting of data that comes under constant scrutiny.

RELATING TO THE WORLD

A significant aspect of women's way of knowing deals with women's connection with the environment. Mother Nature is not named whimsically; women really do make connections with the earth and tend to see it as an evolving and dynamic force. Likewise, women tend to see knowledge as a context-embedded identity that has an impact on the world. Some of the perspectives that feminist scholarship embraces include:

Time: Women view it in terms of relationship/process rather than in objective units.

Power: is seen as limitless rather than zero-sum.

Leadership: is a task of facilitation rather than power and influence.

Individual: needs are considered more important than rules.

The world: is something to live with, not exploit (Miller).

WOMEN'S SCHOLARSHIP

Learning leads into scholarship as researchers delve into underlying principles and construct new theories. The traditional approach in scholarship has been an objective, field-independent, controlled experimental mode:

a model typically embraced by males. However, this is only *one* approach, and not necessarily the most effective method. According to feminist scholarship (Hannigan), as women pursue knowledge they realize the perspectives that each person brings. Therefore, they believe that each person should test assumptions and examine each source's biases and values as s/he researches knowledge. The basic tenet is that knowledge is constructed from multiple perspectives, embedded in society, so that a rich and socially accurate picture will evolve with the inclusion of varied points of view, not only of high-achievers but from the populace at large as well. Feminist scholarship also believes that knowledge is constructed from relations and related thinking, not just from abstract interpretations. Feminist scholarship also recognizes the need to be aware of gender, ethnicity, and class realities.

WHEN WORLDS COLLIDE

What happens when women's ways of knowing conflict with patriarchal approaches to learning? Several issues are at stake in this confrontation, the main ones being power and status. In general, the main set of social rules is in the hands of males, and women need to know them. The question is whether women need to follow them. French notes that when women act like men, they do not always get the same treatment as their male counterparts. If women play the traditional role set forth in male rules, they sometimes feel relegated to second fiddle. If, on the other hand, women play by their own rules, men may find it difficult to relate because they usually do *not* know women's game plans.

As long as the two genders remain ignorant of each other's norms or deny that differences exist, they may apply their own norms to their counterparts and find someone lacking — either themselves or the other gender. They are also likely to treat the other gender as objects or stereotypes rather than as individual human beings.

As women become aware of their own power and freedom of choice, they may feel a sense of loss rather like grieving because they are no longer confined to comfortable, if stifling, traditional roles. They sometimes express rage and anger about their prior inequitable treatment. If they become political, they may go through a period of militancy. Obviously, such behavior does not go unnoticed by the opposite sex.

If uncomfortable with a new or different set of social roles and relations, either sex may revert to traditional stereotypes of behavior. Thus, one of the reactions to the seventies feminist movement was a backlash of opinion and a reaffirmation of the Male Principle (Faludi). Interestingly, as teenage girls begin to be more self-assertive because of gender awareness and belief in gender equity, some adults start longing for the days of sweet young things.

Changing attitudes and behaviors can also be a depressing experience. Women find that they can't do it all. Both men and women have to reprioritize their time and values, which can affect their relationship. Both sexes may have to give up some social privileges such as free dates or "favors." Women may find that they can no longer hide behind the mask of victimization; they have to fend for themselves more. Men have to face shared power situations.

Ultimately, though, empowerment for both sexes should facilitate understanding and acceptance. By learning how different people think and act, both genders can make good use of those varied perspectives and talents to benefit all. The planet really is big enough for the two genders to coexist equitably. And it is up to today's educators to provide a varied set of learning opportunities that encompasses a broad range of learning styles and research methodologies so students can explore their own inner variations as well as those outside their immediate circle.

Chapter 4

The Learning Community

The first problem for all of us, men and women, is not to learn, but to unlearn. — Gloria Steinem

CREATING THE INCLUSIVE, GENDER-EQUITABLE COMMUNITY

Gender issues exist in every school, even single-sex ones: the question is how they are dealt with. Even if schools ignore these issues, that is one way to react to them (it may indicate ignorance, "denial," or a dysfunctional environment). With awareness of gender issues comes the potential for greater sensitivity and acceptance of responsibility to improve the learning situation. Behaviors that were ignored before become glaring. Omissions stand out more with awareness. The following model, adapted from Jackson and Hardiman's work on multicultural organizations, provides a spectrum of school practices relative to gender issues, and can be used to help assess the state of a school culture.

(1) **Exclusion.** Macho Senior High School is a male citadel where the boys are men, and the women are girls. The administration and department heads are all male, and the secretaries are all women. Men teach the "hard" sciences, and women teach the domestic sciences. The few women teachers are all married, largely because their salaries are half of that of their male counterparts. However, no one complains because the principal tends to fire anyone who disagrees with him and his policies. Literature is based on the writings of dead white males. Teaching is done by lecture, and aggressive male behavior is encouraged as girls fold their hands in silence. Sex education occurs only in home economics classes, which is limited to girls, and in back seats of guys' cars. The student leaders are always males, except for the secretary position (held by the President's popular girlfriend). The school is proud of its athletic program: the Warriors. Twelve male teams exist; girls (called the Squaws) play only intramural badminton. The all-girl cheerleader club is known for being very available to the male athletes for very personal

29

attention. Most of the boys go to college; most of the girls get married right after graduation, unless they get pregnant before then.

This school fosters a power system where males dominate women. Decision-makers tend to be males. Male perspectives prevail in textbooks and other sources. Boys are openly favored in classes and student activities. The old-boy network is the way to get things done, and women who seek power or status are undermined.

The effect of this learning environment is substantial. The message is clear: males are first class citizens and females are second-class citizens. Women feel powerless, and suffer loss of self-esteem. Both genders are constrained in rigid roles, and have little opportunity for flexibility or full self-realization. As a result, many good minds are not used, and reactionary behaviors are reinforced.

(2) **Club Mentality**. Ivy High School is considered the rock foundation of the town. Known for providing a Basics education, the school has a strong male principal and a teaching staff with an average of thirty years' experience. New teachers quickly learn what the norms are; the school culture is well established. Little counseling or career guidance is offered; most students follow their fathers' career paths. Courses are open to all students, but girls very seldom take technical arts or computer classes. Attendance at football games is high in comparison to other sports; girls' teams are seldom covered in the school's newspaper. T.G.I.F. is a tradition after school for the principal and his colleagues. Over pitchers of beers the guys review the school week and talk about issues that need to be resolved. Once in a while a couple of single women teachers come along; then the talk is mainly social banter.

This school does not seek to push down women and girls, but it makes no special effort to include them either, except in token ways. The image of the school is one of "doing it the right way: our way." Either a tacit or overt "understanding" exists about appropriate behavior, and it is usually male-directed. Education tends to be traditional.

In this case, traditional social norms dictate the learning community's expectations. There is little room for innovation. As a result, students are not encouraged to break down mental barriers or take intellectual risks. They learn what their elders have learned rather than challenge the status quo.

(3) **Compliance**. Strictly Junior High School prides itself on being gender-blind. All classes are open to all students, but no recruitment is done to encourage cross-gender attendance. Hiring is done without regard to gender. Classes generally have a good balance of males and females, although males still take more advanced math and computer classes than females. Both male and female significant figures are studied across the curriculum,

although no effort is made to study "the common people." Neither students nor teachers are aware of any sex discrimination, and no effort is made to highlight gender issues. Emphasis is on the "team player," and the organization as a whole doesn't want to rock the boat.

This school follows the letter of the law, though not necessarily the spirit of the law, relative to gender issues. The typical approach to learning is to treat everyone the same, not to point out differences. The assumption is that the organization is fine, that changing a few faces will take care of problems.

The limitation of this approach is that the community probably doesn't have ownership in gender issues; a quick fix attitude is in place. As a result, students don't take full advantage of the unique contributions of different persons. In addition, students may find themselves under-prepared when the time comes to deal with gender issues in the work force.

(4) **Affirmative Action.** Forward Middle School's faculty has several new faces, most of whom are female and about a third of whom are people of color; the older group tends to be comprised of Anglo males. Leadership roles are gender-balanced, and all have "paid their dues" to reach the top. The athletic club is coed, as is the cheerleading squad. All students have many opportunities to lead and participate. Courses try to include a balanced perspective, including both genders and different socioeconomic groups. All staff have had an inservice workshop on sexual harassment and one on cooperative learning.

This type of school actively wants to end sexual discrimination and support females. Basically, the system wants to remove the bad practices, but it doesn't glorify those who differ from the norm. It's a learning community that believes "we're all in it together."

Students in this situation know what is expected of them, that all people are considered equal and deserve respect. It is a safe environment for them, with known boundaries. However, students are not encouraged to push the learning "envelope."

(5) **Restructuring.** Change High School has been doing some heavy thinking and discussion — and action. Faculty, students and parents have developed educational initiatives to specifically address gender and equity issues. The Board is reviewing a possible women's studies course; units within the existing curriculum examine gender issues actively. One section of physics contains only girls so they will have a better chance to succeed. In general, girls are encouraged to lead and model classroom behavior. Staff development includes inservice workshops on equitable teaching strategies and alternative learning styles. The school newspaper features gender-related articles, and the halls are abuzz with gender-based discourse.

This school is pursuing gender/equity issues throughout its system, from governance to curriculum to teaching and learning options. It starts questioning basic cultural/social assumptions about learning, and explores the benefits of gender-diverse education. The emphasis is on conscious system-wide self-examination.

In this environment, students can acknowledge differences and talk about them. Learning is dynamic and may be somewhat confrontational as people begin to question tradition. Risk-taking is a part of the educational scene, and no one takes gender issues lying down.

(6) **Gender-Diversity**. Paradise Upper School presents an open and exciting learning atmosphere. New and seasoned teachers, many of whom are female and ethnically diverse, plan innovative courses; interdisciplinary, project-based activities are the norm. Social barriers do not exist; in fact, students regularly meet in faculty homes for elective seminars and club activities. Gender issues are integral throughout the curriculum, and the perspectives of all kinds of people are valued. Source material emphasizes primary documents and different forms of information. Grading is done by authentic assessment. Girls assume leadership roles regularly, and feel safe about taking risks in order to reach their full potential. Peer counseling and tutoring are strong programs within the school.

This school mirrors the contributions of both sexes, and affirms all types of people and learning. The school community does not tolerate oppression in any form. At this stage, inclusiveness and a celebration of diversity are internalized as well as played out daily.

Students in this community have realistic expectations of themselves and others, and welcome the opportunity to help each other grow and contribute fully. All feel proud of their own backgrounds and are eager to expand their knowledge base through mutual interdependent support.

The goal is to reach level six: a gender-diversity empowered learning community. The most convincing evidence of equity occurs when the school's message is aligned with its actions: everyone believes in gender-equity, communicates that message, and lives it. This evolving stage fosters truly authentic learning.

THE CHANGE PROCESS

Change should be considered a normal part of school since learning is, in fact, a change in behavior. However, systemic change within schools typically is not sought after. Frankly, while change is an exciting process, it is a disquieting one as well. We know that even change for the good, such as a promotion or happy marriage, involves self-doubt and some discomfort and readjustment. If a school enjoys its comfortable status, even if it is highly dysfunctional, it is hard for it to move into disequilibrium and seemingly chaotic change.

Note that for systemic change to occur, the whole school and its constituents should be involved. Otherwise, gender issues can become one group's problem, not the system's responsibility. Typically, not everyone will give gender issues equal priority. Nor will every facet of the school be at the same point along the continuum. The particular issues and ways of dealing with them will differ, down to the individual or resource. However, the school as a system needs to have an overarching goal and direction that can connect the efforts of each part of the whole; the structure for supporting and facilitating change needs to be evident to all.

Self-Examination and Diagnosis

Thus, the process of school-wide self-examination is the first step towards achieving the ideal goal of a gender-equitable learning environment, for it accomplishes two objectives: (1) it establishes a baseline for ongoing assessment and (2) it validates the school's awareness of its status, even if it decides not to change at all. No matter where a school lies along the gender-equity continuum, it can feel good that it is acknowledging gender-equity issues.

The corollary, and more significant, activity is to determine *why* the school is at a particular point. Here are some of the factors that can determine a school's status, along with some indicators for each level:

Mission: What is the school's purpose? What is the school trying to accomplish? What strategies does it use?

School culture: What are the school's norms; to what degree are they enforced? What are the overt and covert common beliefs that shape school action? How is the culture established, and how has it evolved?

Curriculum: What is the scope and sequence? How is content articulated and coordinated? What skills, knowledge, and attitudes are being taught?

Material resources: What is the quantity and quality of texts and other educational sources available? What is the library collection? How is technology incorporated? What kinds of supplies are available for staff and students?

Facilities: How does the architecture carry out the school's mission? In what condition are facilities maintained?

Faculty and administration: What quantity and caliber of educators implement the school's mission? How are relationships among teachers, support staff, and administration characterized? How are relationships between educators and students/community members characterized?

Instructional methods/delivery systems: What methods of instruction are utilized, under what conditions? How are instructional decisions made? How does instruction match with student needs and interests? How does scheduling carry out the school's mission?

Community: What role does the community play? How is that role implemented?

Decisionmaking structure and practice: How are decisions characterized? What kind of decisions are made? Who makes decisions? On what basis are decisions made? To what extent are decisions implemented and followed through? What is the relationship between structure and practice?

Standards and assessment: What are the expectations for student outcomes, and how are they developed? How does the school community know that standards are being met? Who assesses; what is assessed; how is assessment done?

Accountability system: How are the school and its elements held accountable? What are the consequences?

The following table provides some indicators at the two extremes of the model's spectrum for each factor:

LEVEL 1 (Exclusion)	LEVEL 6 (Gender-Diversity)
Mission	
No mission; no clear purpose	Strong mission statement which everyone supports
School culture	
Rigid, outdated norms	Open, positive norms which have evolved through whole-community consensus
Curriculum	
Arbitrary, incomplete curriculum without connection to other courses or grades	Cohesive, comprehensive scope and sequence K-14; many options including cross-disciplinary courses
Material resources	
Worn, outdated texts; no library; no non-print sources	Extensive library and resources which address individual needs; fully integrated technology
Facilities	
Cramped, decaying conventional classrooms; no labs	Well-maintained, attractive spaces that support school's activities
Faculty and administration	
Poorly trained, burned-out, understaffed group	Highly prepared and motivated, diverse group; good faculty-student ratio

Instructional methods/delivery systems

Lecture and rote memorization

Well-planned schedule with options for time frames and course structure; wide variety of teaching methods to fit content and needs

Community

Alienated, hostile community

Supportive, involved community who help determine all major policies and directions

Decision-making structure and practice

Hypocritical, authoritative, arbitrary, lone decisionmaker

Site-based, comprehensive-based, decisionmaking body with fair checks and balances

Standards and assessments

No clear student outcomes (graduation by body count), arbitrary and unfair assessments

Authentic, realistic, comprehensive student outcomes, indicators and assessment tools

Accountability system

No accountability

All aspects accountable; broad-based criteria and evaluators insure fair accountability and means to improve

---

Setting Goals: Strategies for Change

Once the school system can describe its present situation, it can determine its goals — and the direction it needs to take in order to achieve those ideals. The assessment can indicate the subsystems that need improvement; further analysis can determine why the situation exists and what obstacles must be overcome in order to change. In addition, the school needs to determine what resources are available to make change happen. With that knowledge, workable strategies can be developed to facilitate positive change. Here are some possible scenarios:

• Students of all types may be able to run for office or develop special-interest groups, but they may not be aware of these possibilities. Inaccurate *perception* is the obstacle, which can be overcome by publicizing student opportunities, actively encouraging girls and other underrepresented groups to take on leadership positions, and reinforcing pro-active student participation.

• The community may have little interest or involvement in the school, and not depend on the school for setting a positive tone. *Attitude and low expectations* are the obstacles. The school can reach out to the community by forming a local council with community members, speaking to and joining

civic groups, asking the community to speak to students, providing community education opportunities, involving community members in policy decisionmaking, and creating opportunities for student connections with the community through internships, curricular projects, and service. Expectations are raised, as is the quality of education delivered.

   • Classes are all self-contained, and no team-teaching or collaborative learning exists. *Structural* changes may be called for. Scheduling can be revamped to facilitate innovative teaching and learning methods.

As seen above, change can affect individuals, the organization, or even the environment. As the reasons for the status quo are ferreted out, a school may find obstacles that seem too overwhelming; breaking them down into composite pieces may help to ameliorate the situation. In other cases, obstacles may be insurmountable, at least in the short run. For example, an existing building structure might impede open classrooms. A strong conservative faculty and community may question or tone down possible sweeping changes. The changes being planned should be realistic and feasible.

This road map of change should also include benchmark critical points along the way, and the strategies to arrive at them. This incremental change process can ease the pains of adjustment and help constituents recognize their own achievements.

Regardless of the particular situation, assessment and planning for change needs to involve the key stakeholders in the school. Especially when gender issues are the heart of the problem, males and females need to be equitably represented — and included in the decisionmaking. Basically, the *model* for change should reflect the type of change desired. Thus, the school that wants to be more gender-equitable in the classroom should also institute inclusive decisionmaking structures that respect and utilize women's input and planning.

Conscious Change

The change process does not occur without discomfort. Getting off the status quo implies being off-balance, at least in terms of systematic equilibrium. Even Columbus had to forego the comforts of the settled Old World, and wrestle with the stormy seas, in order to reach a golden New World. Likewise, conflict must be seen as an inevitable and necessary part of change. By bringing up points of disagreement, the school community can address underlying issues and agendas openly and professionally.

Besides the situation-specific obstacles to change, some generic qualms accompany change:

   • **ignorance** of the present or the future
   • **fear** of the unknown

- comfort of, or respect for, the known **past**
- **denial** of existing problems
- prior negative **experience** relative to change
- lack of **time and other resources**.

Fortunately, some generic factors help relieve or assuage such disequilibrium:

- a shared, clear and articulate **vision** of the desired goal and flexible strategies to get there
- consistent and broad-based **communication** about the change and how to achieve it
- **open and inclusive atmosphere** that encourages risk-taking and sharing
- adequate and thorough **training** so constituents can prepare for change
- **administrative management and support** through release time, adequate space, necessary resources, and compensation for implementing change (Krimmelbein, p. 28; Farmer, 1995, p. 4.7).

In any case, change begins on a tentative and self-conscious level. People may feel awkward as they try new practices. They need the time to adjust, to make mistakes, to regather their energy to persist in the change. Even the act of outwardly following new behaviors does not necessarily mean that inward change occurs; raising an objecting voice may be intimidating and people may go through the motions without changing their personal convictions. Administration needs to listen and be sensitive to individual concerns; conflicting values must be discussed honestly and resolved. People must get to the point that the new approaches become comfortable and routine so they can refine those new methods until they are integrated and internalized.

Institutionalization

For change to become institutionalized, it must be understood and accepted at all levels as the norm. Indeed, the school community's mindset must reflect the new perspective. From hiring procedures to classroom practice, from parent meetings to student rallies, the message and the actions have to be consistent both within the school and in the community at large. At this stage, the system is in equilibrium again, only now the culture embraces different values from before. Backsliding may occur, but the support system and group expectations should be strong enough to bring people back into the now-established revised mainstream.

Of course, the status quo cannot endure forever. Especially if the change has been positive, a school will probably be more open to future change, be

more flexible, and more apt to encourage further improvement. In a way, the change process itself will become a norm: the mark of a true learning community.

LEVELS OF SCHOOL COMMUNITY

Gender equity and student empowerment must be addressed at each level of school involvement. While some efforts can occur at any one level, the whole school must support these ideas if they are to have real meaning and effectiveness. At each level, the associated group needs to undergo the classic model of change examined above. As each of the following levels is discussed, questions are posed to stimulate critical thinking and guide in that assessment.

The School as a Whole

The school community is a microcosm of the world and, as such, models the expectations that society wants students to have in order to participate as adults. Now it may be asserted that since gender inequity exists in the real world, students should be prepared to live in that condition. That approach assumes a status quo society. However, if education is about helping youth develop their full potential and helping them become life-long learners, then it behooves schools to show students the social reality *and* to help students find solutions to improve that society. Thus, schools should affirm and live out the concept of the learning community, a safe place to take educational risks as young people explore their environment and themselves.

What does such a learning community look like? Some indicators follow:

a sense of inclusion: everyone is respected, and everyone participates according to skill and interest

a sense of family: everyone plays an important role and is interdependent, and everyone feels safe and supported

a holistic attitude: behaviors, thoughts, and feelings are intertwined and valued; curriculum reflects the whole person

a sense of authenticity: assessment and teaching relate to multi-faceted performance; learning connects each person meaningfully with her/himself and the world.

What the Administration Can Do

School site administrators in general, and the principal in particular, really do set the tone for the school and its treatment of gender issues. Not

only their decisions, but also their decisionmaking process, indicate their values about gender. For example, if the old-boys network runs the school, then probably sexually discriminatory practices will occur, and students will quickly learn those same biases. If inclusive group processing characterizes school practice, then students will more likely imitate that model and apply it in their own lives. If sexual harassment is tolerated at any level, credibility in gender equity is lost. If, on the other hand, significant affirmative actions for the youngest student to the oldest staff exemplify school life, then the community will get the message that gender equity and empowerment of all is real.

How do administrators work with *staff*?

Who generally gets hired; what gender-linked trends occur?

What role does staff development play; does everyone have a level playing field to work from?

Who advances on the school career ladder — and why?

Is there an active staff union; what is its position on gender equity?

What is the general tone of the staff: inclusive or exclusionary and territorial?

While all the staff have to "buy" into the concept of gender equity and student empowerment, the administration needs to provide the vision to inspire the group and the muscle to help guide the change process for the better. Administrators can model gender-inclusionary behavior by seeking out diverse potential faculty from local teacher-preparatory institutions, and by encouraging existing faculty to test innovative practices that foster gender-equitable learning. Administrators can rotate leadership roles to ensure that all faculty have a chance to exhibit and expand their professional repertoire. Active mentorship programs can be instituted for all faculty. Administrators can invite staff families to school functions, and make accommodations for those staff members needing to deal with family situations. The underlying atmosphere should be one of acceptance and use of diverse talents among the staff.

On a more immediate level, administrators set the tone for *student action* relative to gender equity.

Are youth included in school task forces and policy groups?

Is the student body a viable decisionmaking entity with clout?

Are both genders equally represented in these leadership roles?

In a gender-inclusive school, the student body government would be likely to be active and credible. Administration can ensure that students are represented on school decisionmaking committees. Administration can guide scheduling so that it accommodates a wide variety of options to engage the interests and use the varied talents of the entire school population. Administration can also set the tone for student/faculty collaboratory relationships that promote active learning.

A major job of administration is to deal with the *community* at large.

Do open lines of communication exist between school and the rest of the community?

Does the school include the community in its educational and co-curricular offerings?

Is the community represented on decisionmaking bodies?

A holistic, relationist attitude is a mark of women's approach to learning; school and the rest of life blend. This blurring of school-community edges affects both staff and students, and administrators should be sensitive to it. For instance, personal hobbies can enrich the school experience; teachers and students might display or perform their creations. Family connections can be affirmed; sample activities include class presentations and fundraising. Staff and students might bring in their offspring (yes, teens do have children). Responsibilities to offspring and older family members need to be recognized and accommodated by administrators.

How the Co-Curricular
Environment Can Reflect Gender-Equity

Substantial learning also occurs outside the classroom, within the school structure. Adolescents, in particular, need opportunities to belong to a group, to do personally meaningful activity, and to succeed. Co-curricular activities permit young people to choose how to spend their time much more liberally than is possible in the formal curriculum. Moreover, as the school plays a critical role in socializing students, co-curricular activities provide models of social expectations. A variety of activities can reinforce gender stereotypes — or facilitate gender-consciousness and empowerment for all. Co-curricular activities can be scrutinized with regard to gender practices, similarly to the way textbooks are analyzed. The results of that assessment then provide the guide for social change.

Clubs can be examined on a group-by-group basis.

What purpose does a club have, and what activities are involved?

Who belongs, and who leads?

What is the club's popularity and status?

What kind of financial and moral support does it get from the rest of school?

How are efforts recognized both within the club and by the rest of the school?

The status of co-curricular activities, as a whole, should also be examined.

What interests are represented, and which are omitted?

What is the process for establishing a club or school function?

Do participation or leadership positions follow gender lines?

How do students gain leadership skills?

Do club advisors tend to be male or female?

How does the school recognize co-curricular efforts; do awards cross interest lines?

Does the school celebrate women's contributions through activities such as Women's History Month?

Educators can facilitate gender-equitable experiences for student activities. They can encourage all students to participate and lead. They can establish a safe and comforting atmosphere so all students can test ideas and push their own limits in co-curricular activities. A broad mix of faculty should advise activities and support student events so students can learn on an even base with their elders and see their achievements honored by their role models.

Sports play a significant co-curricular role in many schools, and can be considered an accurate indicator of gender equity. Recent studies demonstrate that participation in school sports teams significantly increases girls' esteem just as it does boys'. Yet, by and large, even with Title IX regulations, boys' sports usually enjoy greater community coverage and support. Examining participation numbers, financial support, general popularity, even the quality of uniforms are starting points for improving the status and power of female athletics. (Even the name of a team can indicate gender status. For example, are boys called Eagles and girls called Eaglets? Is this OK? The basis for the decision is as important as the name, for Eaglets could indicate second-class status, or it could emphasize the girls' affirmation of their sex.)

What the Library Media Center Can Offer

As an information center, the library media center is integral to gender equity and empowerment opportunities. The question is "Does the library fulfill that potential?" While the librarian has the final responsibility for developing and implementing an effective plan, the whole school community also participates in its success or frustration; all members need to help plan, support, and evaluate efforts in the library media center.

The most obvious component is *collection development*. Expanding on the classroom experience, the library's collection should be analyzed in terms of gender issues.

Is representation adequate, fair, and multi-faceted?

Can every student find a positive role model somewhere in the collection?

Do primary sources abound, telling the story of both famous and not-so-famous people?

Do materials mirror the variety of learning styles, and thus include a rich assortment of print and non-print items?

Is equipment adequate so all resources can be physically accessed?

Since students need to access information intellectually as well as physically, the library teacher must ensure viable **instruction** that incorporates gender sensitivity. Beyond the questions posed to the classroom teacher, the library teacher must answer issues about alternative ways of delivery: signage, guidesheets, posters, displays, videotapes, audiocassette tapes, computer tutorials. Each mode needs to reflect gender-consciousness, and the composite group of instructional aids should reflect the variety of student needs.

Other services besides instruction exist in the library, and should facilitate student empowerment.

Do readers' advisory and other reading encouragement expand gender roles or stereotype them?

Do displays show a variety of positive options for both genders?

Do programs help attendees gain insights about themselves and each other?

Do contests encourage collaboration as well as competition?

Do facilities for producing information-based presentations favor one sex over another?

Is computer use equitable? (In some settings, specific times may be blocked out for girls' use only as a way to ensure fair access.)

Even the *space* allocation within the library media center relays a message about gender bias or equity.

Do areas exist for both individual and group work?

Is space divided so students can find a nook or other safe, private space?

Do acoustics permit study buddies who don't disturb other users?

Does the library arrangement, in general, promote interaction with resources?

Does library decor help the student feel welcome and accepted?

Does furniture arrangement facilitate librarian-student interaction?

Students also gain power by *helping in the library*. Those opportunities should reinforce gender-equity consciousness; the library teacher should be an advocate for competent young women. Thus, girls should be as able to fix computers as boys. Boys can do overdues. Both can process materials. Students should be introduced to a number of activities so they can experience possibly heretofore undiscovered ability. (My best book coverer was a 200+ pound African-American sophomore boy.) Training and delegation should also mirror gender-equitable treatment. Adult staff and volunteers should also receive gender-equitable supervision as they both develop their own skills and train students.

All of these functions require effective *management.* The library teacher's own values are revealed by behavior, showing how fairly people are supervised and materials are handled.

Does the management style take advantage of the best of differing philosophies, and provide an inclusive atmosphere for learning?

Do budgetary decisions reflect enlightened competence?

To what degree are facility decisions under the library teacher's control, and do they reveal traditional gender roles?

In fact, does the librarian's management itself reflect authentic authority and valid status within the larger school community? The school librarian's role has traditionally been associated with female clerical skills and mothering abilities such as storytelling. Too often, the rest of the school community does not realize the changes introduced into the library science profession. Administrative and technological competencies are required of today's school librarians, and those high-level responsibilities need to be credited by administrators. We school librarians also need to be more assertive and pro-active in order to ensure that our skills are well used within the school. Female librarians, in particular, need to model the power of information professionals. Strong school librarianship is a testament to the career opportunities for diverse, capable people.

What the Classroom Teacher Can Do

The heart of the school rests with the primary "family" of the school: the teacher and her/his students in a self-contained classroom. (Some efforts have been made for more open learning structures, but the group dynamics and sense of belonging afforded to a traditional classroom are hard to deny.) The classroom provides the most intense opportunity for practicing empowering behaviors; students can get daily reinforcement in a safe environment.

As the classroom teacher and students define themselves and their roles and rules, gender issues should be faced. Teachers need to examine their *own behaviors* in light of gender.

Do they address females differently from males?

Do they give more feedback to males?

Are their expectations gender-linked?

Does discipline differ between the sexes?

Having an outside observer or, even better, a videotape of classroom behavior provides valuable objective feedback. Teachers can then make conscious efforts to model gender-equitable actions. For instance, a variety of teaching strategies can be used to engage students with different learning styles. Teachers can encourage cooperative learning, and devise heterogeneous groups to maximize student opportunities for sharing their unique gifts. Teachers can model bias-free feedback that assesses both content and process for each student, and can provide chances for students to cross-evaluate their peers' efforts. The basic underpinning of the classroom, though, is the overall atmosphere; it should reflect mutual respect, openness, and safe exploration. A rigid authoritative climate can be replaced by a more collegial model.

Students too need to look at their own *behaviors.*

What language do they use with each other?

With whom do they socialize — and why?

What kind of body language do they use?

What does dress communicate?

What are their self-expectations?

Do they support each other?

Besides acting as role models, teachers can help students learn gender-equitable behavior by fostering class discussions about appropriate behaviors. Students and teachers can cooperatively establish normative expectations of actions and attitudes. Students can reinforce those norms among themselves, thus empowering them and moving responsibility for learning onto their shoulders.

The *resources* for learning require critical analysis as well. Textbooks are only the beginning; hopefully, the library media center has a vast array of print and non-print materials that offer insights from a wide spectrum of viewpoints. And hopefully, students have frequent opportunities across the curriculum to use these materials as they make meaningful connections with them. As stated in other parts of this book, the following factors should be examined: content, perspective, representation, images, language. Note that the unifying piece in the classroom is the *curriculum.*

Does it incorporate gender issues and empower all students?

What main concepts drive classwork?

What values do they represent?

What meaning does the curriculum have in students' lives?

How is curriculum implemented?

Do students help determine and plan content and delivery?

Curriculum acts as the stage set for learning; students expand their own repertoire of learning strategies by interacting with meaningful content. Teacher planning and responsiveness to student needs can maximize the effectiveness of curriculum by particularizing the experiences to match the needs of each specific group of students at a given time. The teacher thus acts as an intervener when students need outside help or redirection.

TIPS ON ACHIEVING AN EMPOWERED SCHOOL COMMUNITY

The journey from level 1 exclusion to level 6 gender-diversity is not smooth. It may involve detours, jump-starts, short-cuts, and merges. It requires constant reassessment and realignment. As individuals and organizations experience change, they may also experience discomfort and anxiety. For that reason, committed leadership and a strong support system are needed for effective progress.

The following scenarios offer specific examples of problems and solutions encountered as schools try to become more gender-equitable. Each setting will follow a unique path, but these pointers can act as guideposts that can be adapted to particular situations.

(1) Problem: **Short-circuiting**

Action: The teacher short-circuits student efforts by cutting them off, interfering with their processing, stopping student questions, or completing the student's work.

Typical phrases:

"Let me do that for you."

"Get to the point!"

"Don't interrupt; the last five minutes of class will be question time. Period."

"Wrong, Anne. Jim, tell the class the right answer."

Implication: This action lowers student self-esteem and discourages inquiry. After a while, students will stop independent thinking.

Intervention: The teacher gives students enough time to process; teacher provides prompts so students can discover the answers themselves.

Constructive phrases:

"Let me know if you need some more time to process this."

"I hadn't considered that perspective, Myra. Can you expand on your theory?"

"What do you need in order to complete this task, Derek?"

"We'll take seven minutes to present this information. Then I want you to discuss any questions you have with your partner. I'll clarify your remaining concerns."

(2) Problem: **Stereotyping**

Action: The teacher stereotypes a student's behavior.

Typical phrases:

"I expect you to be good in home ec., Rita. Didn't your mother teach you anything?"

"Well, what do you expect from boys?"

"Carol, you take notes. Hank will lead the discussion."

"Neat-looking paper, Sasha. You wrote some good ideas, Jerrold."

Implication: Students are typed rather than treated as individuals, so have lower self-identities.

Intervention: The teacher becomes aware of generalizations made by her/himself or others, and counters them.

Constructive phrases:

"Everyone, take turns leading your small group and taking notes."

"Janet will show the class how to analyze the gravitation force using vectors."

"Interesting point, Jack. Fascinating concept, Mary."

"Gary, I hear that you cook great omelets. What's your secret?"

(3) Problem: **Diminishment**

Action: The teacher diminishes the student in front of others by being condescending, labeling behavior, or expecting lesser performance

"Girls aren't good at math, so don't worry. I still can't add my checkbook."

"Now aren't we a little old to be acting like that, Emma?"

"Andrew's work is more important than yours, Nancy, so give him your supplies, OK?"

"You're always whining, Josh. Get a life."

Implication: Students have lower self-expectations, and may not feel worthy of attention or care. Some students may rebel or withdraw in defeat.

Intervention: The teacher listens to her/his own statements and those of students; the teacher encourages all students to achieve; the teacher tries not to react impetuously under pressure.

Constructive phrases:

"Give me a minute before I react to that statement."

"Can we talk about this problem privately?"

"You sound frightened, Gary. Tell me why."

"Each person's role in the group has merit. Work as a team and come up with a great solution!"

(4) Problem: **Single-cycle interaction**

Action: Classroom discussion is teacher-controlled, with all conversation going back and forth between the teacher and one student at a time.

Typical phrases:

"What is fructose, Beth?" "Right." "Lee, where is fructose found?" "Wrong. Ned, you answer the question."

"Explain why the South lost the Civil War, Myron." "You forgot about the trade issue. April, tell what impact trade had on the outcome of the Civil War."

Implication: Students depend on the teacher for all learning; processing is blocked.

Intervention: The teacher acts as a facilitator for student learning; students learn in groups and report their findings; students experience leadership roles in groups.

"Go into your discussion groups and reach a consensus about the reasons that the South lost the Civil War. We'll share our findings in the large group."

"How many agree with Sam's answer? Let's have some of you explain your positions."

(5) Problem: **Response etiquette**

Action: Girls raise their hands; boys spontaneously call out answers. Some students never volunteer. Teacher responds more often to assertive students.

Typical phrases:

"Great, Nora. I can count on you to give the right answer."

"Stop that playing around, Darwin, and keep quiet."

"Aaron always tests well. Too bad he doesn't participate in class."

"I don't call on the Rodriguez girls. They just giggle. And the other students don't understand them anyway."

Implication: Some students are overlooked, so good ideas are lost. Teachers may not realize a student's strengths or weaknesses. Mutual respect is not reinforced. Students who need a longer time to process their answers are not acknowledged for their thinking.

Intervention: Determine communication patterns, and make sure all students have a chance to participate; use cooperative learning activities to allow students more chances to share their experiences with others and be heard; provide other means for students with language barriers to demonstrate their knowledge; provide enough wait time so all students can think through their responses.

"Discuss the key facts in small groups. One person in each group is responsible for making sure that everyone gets to talk."

"Turn to your partner, and come up with three follow-up questions. Write them down, and we'll discuss them."

"Rearrange your chairs in a circle so everyone can see each other."

"Marya, call on another student to continue the discussion."

(6) Problem: **Limited communication style**

Action: Differences in ways of talking undercut some people's effectiveness.

Typical phrases:
"Why can't you talk more like Joe?"
"You need to sound more forceful."
"We speak English here. I don't want to hear you talking to your neighbor in Iranian or whatever that language is."
"If you can't talk in complete sentences, don't talk at all."
Implication: Some students' contributions are downplayed; certain expressive styles are reinforced to the detriment of other approaches; cultural backgrounds are dismissed; variations in expressions are lost so students do not expand their repertoires.
Constructive phrases:
"You sound a little tentative, Joyce. Could you expand on your thoughts?"
"Manuel, will you help translate the student discussion? You can help me understand too."
"That's one way to express that idea, Wayne. Gloria, how would you describe that concept?"
"We'll be exploring different ways to convey ideas: by debate, through poetry, in dramatic form, and by persuasive essay."

(7) Problem: **Under-representation**
Action: Student leadership does not reflect gender and ethnic representation in the school.
Typical phrases:
"You can't be a cheerleader. Guys don't wear skirts."
"I can see why you feel weird in the computer club; you're the only girl. Perhaps you should drop out."
"Why would you join the multicultural club? You're not black."
"I notice boys seem to run all the clubs. I guess they're just natural leaders."
Implication: Under-represented groups feel alienated and do not learn leadership skills.
Intervention: Focus groups discuss the reasons for under-representation and develop solutions; girls and other under-represented groups are given leadership workshops; leadership roles are extended in different arenas; students are elected to represent different groups; leadership roles are not dependent on gender characteristics (especially in sports).
Constructive phrases:
"Have you considered getting other girls to sign up for the small engines class, Jill? I'll help you if you wish."
"There's a real need for more girls to conduct class meetings. Let's plan a workshop to teach students how to facilitate groups, and encourage some girls to attend."

"Let's brainstorm some ways to include a greater diversity of students in sports."

(8) Problem: Avoidance
Action: School staff are uncomfortable with gender issues.
Typical phrases:
"We don't have a problem. There's no difference between boys and girls."
"I think sex belongs in the privacy of one's bedroom, not in the schools."
"What's wrong with flirting? You just have a hang-up."
"Let the home ec classes deal with it."
Implication: Students do not become aware of gender issues and don't learn how to deal with them.
Intervention: Staff and administration have workshops on gender issues; staff examine the school's philosophy and teaching methods; curriculum addresses gender issues.
Constructive phrases:
"This may be an uncomfortable topic, but we have to face it so our students will be well-prepared and self-confident."
"How can we integrate gender issues across the curriculum?"
"Gus has great success working with students on self-initiated projects. Could you share your insights, Gus?"
"I've felt excluded and intimidated because I'm a gay teacher. I think the administration needs to examine their practices. Could a committee be set up to seek some positive solutions?"

(9) Problem: Exclusionary associations
Action: Faculty associate with their own kind, either by gender, ethnicity, or department.
Typical phrases:
"Well, you know the science department. They're always against rallies."
"Do you notice how it's always the same teachers who get on committees?"
"The Latino teachers seem to have a private running joke among themselves. I wonder what it is."
"I'd like to join the guys for a beer after school, but I'm afraid they'd think I was cramping their style."
Implications: Staff do not learn how to associate and work with people who are different.
Intervention: Mix groups for activities: do intergroup training and role-playing on diversity. Administrators should be gender-conscious as they hire and advance teachers.

"I'd like one representative from each department to be on the committee. Make sure it's someone who hasn't served before."

"Our goal this year is to recruit a broader-based faculty pool who reflect our student population."

"We're having an all-faculty picnic. You can bring your families too."

"To encourage cross-disciplinary teaching, the Site Council will provide team-teachers with an extra prep period to ensure success."

(10) Problem: **Isolationism**
Action: The school does not link with the community in its efforts to become
    gender-equitable.
Typical phrases:
"Involving the community will just confuse the issue."

"I don't want parents running the school. I don't tell them how to run their business."

"Our plates are full enough already. We don't have time to mess with the community."

"Let students get part-time jobs after school if they want career exploration. Our job is to teach the curriculum."

"Maybe we should just abolish Open House. The parents aren't interested anyway."
Implication: Students and staff cannot transfer learning to the outside world.
Intervention: Establish focus groups to examine why the community is not
    connecting with the school; identify interest groups for possible links;
    develop plans for connecting the school and the community; have school
    members join community groups.
Constructive phrases:
"Let's set up some focus groups to brainstorm ways to involve parents in their students' education."

"Which faculty members volunteer in the community or have relatives who work locally? We could use their input."

"Could we establish a list of community people who would be willing to speak to classes or provide internships for students?"

"We could volunteer the school facilities for community education. Perhaps some teachers would lead evening courses or suggest names of possible community instructors."

Chapter 5

Women's Studies and Information Skills

Nothing in life is to be feared. It is only to be understood.
— Madame Curie

GAINING CONTROL

"Information is power." A more accurate truism would be "The *use* of information is power." Young people, especially females, may feel powerless, so meaningful coping techniques help them feel capable and in control. Particularly in this era of data, library/information skills allow youth to explore different options and make reasoned decisions that can affect their lives.

This chapter examines major information skills, and uses gender issues as a content focus for gaining knowledge and solving problems.

INCLUSIVE WAYS AND INFORMATION SKILLS

As the examples below will illustrate, information skills are seen as tools and information literacy is context-embedded, just as a needle isn't very useful to study unless used to sew, remove splinters, or otherwise manipulate. A basic tenet in feminist scholarship (and in other methodologies as well) is that students *construct* knowledge by gathering data in a variety of ways from a variety of perspectives. They consciously examine the values and beliefs in which information is embedded, and incorporate those perspectives into the total multifaceted and ever-changing picture.

Moreover, information skills can be seen as relational. Students find relationships between pieces of information, they relate information to themselves, and they relate information to the world around them. This connecting provides a deeper meaning to the information found, and engages the whole person.

INFORMATION SKILLS AND PROBLEM SOLVING

One image to use when thinking of information skills is that of problemsolving. This grounds the process in real-life terms:

- What is the problem?
- What are the underlying issues?
- What are the facts?
- What are the options?
- What are the consequences?
- What is the best outcome?
- How good was the decision?

Using a problemsolving construct can also make it easier for students to confront gender issues because it can acknowledge present perceptions and encourage a broader range of possibilities that can be acted upon. By approaching information skills as problemsolving techniques, students become empowered to make a difference, both intellectually and psychologically.

Relating to information involves a series of tasks, which are outlined below. Each requires meaningful intellectual and psychological engagement, each helps solve problems, and each can deal with gender-sensitive content.

#1: Task Definition

"What am I supposed to do?" "What is the problem?" These may be the hardest questions to answer. Teachers need to have a clear idea what they want their students to accomplish, and they need to explain their expectations clearly. Students should be encouraged to ask clarifying questions. Females in particular need to feel safe to ask for clarification. Student tasks are also made more focused if the students have experienced similar tasks before, so they should be encouraged to link the present task with past learning as a way to find defining relationships.

The easiest way to *define the task or problem* is to show an example of it. Too often students have to fish around for the correct answer. While teachers sometimes object to the question "How long does it have to be?", they should realize that students usually are trying to get a handle on the assignment. Why should they have to guess or play mastermind with the teacher? Good teaching includes accurate modeling; this approach works for research tasks as well.

Once students understand the task and have a model or goal to work for, they can determine *what kind of information* they need to complete the task or solve the problem. A simple, yet often overlooked, preparatory task is to have students list (1) what information they know already, and (2) what they don't know. In some cases, the content may assume gender stereotypes or ignore gender differences. A research project on same-sex relationships may be approached in entirely different ways depending on the students' gender or lifestyle.

If students have prior experience with resources, they can focus on the specific task or new critical feature more easily. In some cases, students don't have the necessary past experiences to enable them to focus on the content at hand. For instance, suppose a physics assignment requires students to analyze the different forces that make a motorcycle run. If students haven't spent much time around such vehicles, they will feel lost or not know how to do the fact-finding process efficiently.

In addition, students need to select the critical factors in the *process* in order to guide their thinking about choosing information sources. For example, if the teacher asks students to compare two perspectives on a recent event, students should pick out the words "compare," "perspectives," and "recent event." Students could then infer that articles from two different periodicals would provide the needed information. As with prior knowledge about content, students may also differ in their information processing skills. A project may call for small groups to develop a skit about the immigration experience. Girls may have more experience working in cooperative groups than boys, or they may have an easier time creating skits. In short, determining information requires that the teacher help students with those prerequisite skills of analyzing a task and linking likely sources of information to that task.

Thus, teachers and students need to assess what *preliminary content and information skills* need to be taught before the lesson's main task can be accomplished and the problem can be solved.

#2: Research Strategies

At this point students must figure out how to find what they need in order to do the task or solve the problem. Usually this requires exploring a series of elements to cover the topic at hand. Teachers can help students develop this skill by providing them with sample strategies or frameworks. One example follows:

(1) Get background information on the topic from encyclopedias.
(2) Determine key words.
(3) Define terms using dictionaries.
(4) Use access tools such as indexes and catalogs.
(5) Find in-depth information in books.

(6) Find facts in specialized reference sources.
(7) Find current information, if needed, in periodicals and databases.
(8) Locate alternative sources such as videos, pamphlets, etc.
(9) Periodically review and revise the research question and key words.
(10) Alternate between general information and specific facts.
(11) Use one source as a springboard to another source.
(12) Research related fields.

It must be noted that this structure has a sequential feel. Boys tend to be more comfortable with this approach. Many girls, however, may feel constrained or stymied by a step-by-step approach. Teachers can help assuage this situation by creating a separate display card for each element and presenting them en masse, holistically, rather than in step fashion. They may also model a searching strategy that alternates between elements as new associations spring forth. Another approach is to discuss with students how one problem leads to another problem, ultimately generating a web of issues and consequences.

Students can make personal notes for each step or otherwise document their work. Information mapping or webbing allows students to show how ideas relate. Drawings or diagrams can help students visualize the information and make it their own. Student recordings should include those resources and strategies that were *not* useful, as well as those that were; this encourages safe risk-taking, which girls may need to experience more. The underlying idea is that even a "wrong" source provides valuable insight; the student knows one avenue *not* to pursue.

For major tasks or units, students need several sessions to accomplish their work. Ideally, at the end of each session students should review and share their strategies. In this way, they can suggest ideas for others and receive new insights from their peers. Particularly if most work is done individually, this process time allows for group support. If research is done cooperatively, then the group needs to process their session's work as a means of evaluating their progress. Using the problemsolving image, students can share clues and set up more ways to dig into the "case."

#3: Locating and Accessing Information

Two levels for each sub-task are needed. First, students need to decide how to locate the information, how to find the facts. In the research process, students may consult some kind of index or catalog as a first step in order to find the source itself. The research step of key words is essential here since many indexes use a controlled vocabulary to organize the indexed sources. It should be noted that computerized indexes and catalogs rely less on this abstraction step. The second sub-task is to find the resource itself. Students need to be reminded, particularly with periodicals indexes, that the library media center may not have the suggested resource — but that they can use other libraries.

Traditional research has concentrated on sequential, factual print material. Such narrowly defined resources do not address the learning styles and interests of many students. Thus, teachers need to value and encourage the use of non-print resources. They may be materials such as videos and CD-ROMs, or they may be human resources, either at school or in the community. These sources can be harder to locate, partly due to the, again, traditional emphasis on print. Libraries sometimes have catalogs of union collections of non-print materials and speakers' or organizational directories to help find experts in the field.

Physically accessing the information within the source is a separate procedure. For books, students need to look at both table of contents and indexes (the former usually if the topic is broad, the latter if a specific fact is being researched). As students try to find specifics, they should also look at the source's arrangement of information, i.e., alphabetically, chronologically, or thematically.

Non-print materials pose different access situations. CD-ROMs often include random-access searching software. Videos, on the other hand, usually require sequential scanning. Humans need to be interviewed or surveyed, which demands a separate set of information skills. Interestingly, girls may find themselves the experts in these non-traditional access methods since they are often expected to ascertain non-verbal or literal cues.

A third level may exist: students may find the information but not be able to understand it; they lack *intellectual access*. This gap often exists when the student has little prior experience in the area, and so cannot link the new information to existing knowledge. As girls and boys differ in their upbringing, the issue of intellectual access becomes something more than IQ. For example, some boys may not have as much experience cooking so may lack skill in understanding certain chemical reactions. Teachers may need to take remedial steps to help students decipher the information placed before them. In some cases, students do not have the requisite skills of reading in context (either textually or visually). Being able to "read" interviewees is an even more complex skill, for the student needs to hear the content and tone of the speaker as well as interpret the accompanying body language. Such interpersonal skills may be glossed over by some males — and relished by some females who may be well-versed in relational "data." Ultimately, teachers need to appreciate the fact that locating a source does not equal accessing it, and they need to help students bridge that intellectual gap.

#4: Using Information

Now that the students have the information, can they understand it and use it? That is the next step. They need to *evaluate the source*: what is the perspective, how accurate is it, how thorough is it, how useful is it for the purposes of solving the problem? Students sometimes do not give a critical eye to resources, and instead consider it as "holy script." Teachers need to help students maintain an open approach to the sources, which may be difficult for those who have been conditioned to accept what other people say as authoritative and correct. Again, using the problemsolving image helps since most students would recognize that not all sources of information are equally credible. A useful approach is to question all assumptions; teachers need to emphasize that opinions may differ about a particular point and that the investigator needs to look at the background experience that the chronicler brings to the source material. For instance, how a single mother and an absent father look at child care might be equally valid, considering their perspectives; one cannot automatically discount one viewpoint or the other. If a male doctor and a female doctor interpret symptoms differently, which expert might be regarded more highly? A useful sub-task is content analysis, whereby students examine a source in depth by classifying, tabulating and evaluating its key aspects.

The other major task in using information is to *determine the important facts* relative to the project at hand. Some students have trouble picking out the main ideas. Some intervention methods are simple; when examining a text, for instance, teachers can usually help students by pointing out headings and topic sentences. The more subtle issue, though, is deciding what information is important in light of the topic being researched or problem to be solved. Thus, documents on welfare reform need to be approached differently if the issue is child care or if the issue is tax rebates. In a way, those students who are context-sensitive (usually associated more with females) will probably have an easier time because they can see the connotations as they impact their topic more readily than "field-independent" learners.

Two gender issues are at stake here: the interplay of authority/acceptance, and the response to controversy. Young women may tend to accept the source's validity more than men, not necessarily because they think it is right, but because they see any chronicler as one in power. Girls may also see the relative validity of a person's point of view because their concepts of right vs. wrong may be more situationally sensitive than boys' ideology. That same sense of ambiguous "rightness" may lead to a feminine reluctance to challenge viewpoints; indeed, girls have been socialized to a great extent to harmonize varying opinions rather than to confront them. Boys, on the other hand, traditionally have been given freer rein to fight and debate others. Controversy for them may be seen as an exciting challenge rather than as a nerve-wracking threat. Since both kinds of comparisons, finding similarities *and* differences, provide insight into ideas, boys and girls can teach each other different ways to engage with source material and move towards equity. Conflicting ideas can be viewed as a viable and healthy way to see other points of view and a means to create personally meaningful and valid solutions to gender-sensitive problems.

#5: Synthesizing Information

Once the data-gathering function is done (at least at the first round) and individual findings have been analyzed, then the task of *organizing and integrating information* from those different sources takes place. Students need to find patterns in their data; how do findings and sources relate? Naturally, students need to link their findings to the task definition, but they also need to look at the lateral connections between sources. In terms of problemsolving, students are comparing options to ultimately determine the best outcome. Synthesis is actually one of the most creative aspects of information skills, for it calls on a person's prior experience with trends and patterns, and encourages students to make intuitive, intellectual or psychological connections. Because male and female backgrounds may differ in terms of experiences *and* interpretation of those experiences, mixed-gender learning groups provide a way for all students to broaden their knowledge bases. Just as with note-taking, outlines are perfectly fine for organizing information, and other ways of linking ideas also should be considered: mapping, webs, hypermedia, visuals, etc.

Beyond synthesis and organization lies *presentation*. This latter task requires translating the synthesis into terms that others can understand. On a very practical level, this transformation of information ensures that students understand what they read and make it their own; plagiarism is rarely an issue if meaningful presentation incorporates the transformation of gathered data into an original form. Students should be encouraged to explore alternative means of sharing their information: skits, debates, simulations, multimedia presentations, videos, "white papers," games, and other "real life" applicable modes. Often these presentations are team efforts, which reinforce feminine awareness of relational learning and group responsibility. Such collaborative results can be used to assess social tasks as well as academic ones.

#6: Evaluation

Evaluation occurs on two levels: how well did students produce/behave and how well did the process work (planning, implementation, and assessment)?

This two-faceted approach recognizes the symbiotic relationship involved in information literacy: method and means are intertwined with results and ends. It also recognizes that the best solution to a problem has to take into account the process by which that solution was derived. Girls, who have been traditionally associated with "doing things right," can have their efforts given greater weight relative to intellectual accomplishment.

Students should have opportunities to assess their peers, their teachers, and themselves in terms of process and product. Rigorous and insightful evaluation should take into account both skills and attitudes, to mirror different students' abilities and to foster a broad repertoire of examination methods for both girls and boys. Ideally, students and teachers would develop the relevant rubric at the beginning of the unit, and use it during the activity as well as afterwards to do formative evaluations and make modifications as appropriate.

A good model to use is an art critique whereby the teacher and students all comment on the project. Certain criteria for judgment are first agreed upon, in this case, elements such as composition, style, and technique. The "creators" also explain their project, clarifying their intent and procedure as well as their self-assessment of relative success of the effort. This set-up is also an opportunity to tune into gender issues as they relate to process and product. For instance, gender expectations may influence the choice of subject matter; boys may feel that "still lifes" are sissy, girls may avoid mechanistic artwork. Girls may feel more inhibited than boys in how they use a medium, fearing to make mistakes or look messy. These open critiques allow students to examine their assumptions about the quality of work, and broaden their criteria to embrace a variety of options.

Another key factor in evaluation is "authenticity." Does the evaluation match the intent? Does it measure behavior? Is it real? Again, the closer the assessment is aligned with the real world — and the activity also simulates reality — the greater the chance for internalized and applied learning. The evaluation makes sense because it helps students predict how successful they will be when outside the school walls. Thus a student business plan can be evaluated by actual business people, who could give their judgment about the feasibility of that business surviving. Especially as girls are sometimes "protected" from experimenting in "real-world" conditions, the safe environment of the educational world helps girls connect with the community, simulate life situations, and learn skills that will transfer to later life-dependent problemsolving.

The incorporation of cooperative learning complicates the evaluation, for students need to evaluate the group social task skill as well as the content/information skills. In addition, they must look at both group efforts and individual efforts. This approach reinforces the "team" approach that boys usually engage in through sports and recognizes girls' appreciation of supporting one another. Evaluation may be more holistic than detailed, or the evaluators can pinpoint one or two unique, worthwhile issues to evaluate and not "grade" the other factors. This approach frees both genders to try non-stereotypical behaviors without too much risk; boys can be reinforced for giving nurturing statements, and girls can be encouraged to speak out more.

Evaluation should also signal the start of the *next* activity. In other words, where do we go from here? Hopefully, the activity stimulates more questions that need answering or at least exploring, just as the solution to one problem often leads to another problem. The more students and teachers can together plan that learning journey, the more meaningful the experience. In addition, joint planning places more control in the hands of the students so they feel more respected. Furthermore, when skills build on one another *naturally*, as natural outcomes of prior learning, transfer of knowledge is easier — and more substantial. Especially for the students who categorize or separate each learning experience (often boys), the skill of relating material is a valuable lesson in itself.

THINKING ABOUT THINKING

Throughout the process of learning and using information skills to solve problems, students should take time to reflect on the processes they use. In a way, research provides an abstract simulation of the personal quest that each person undergoes when growing up. Students encounter obstacles and the unknown, and they must overcome or incorporate those issues through conscious decisionmaking and reflection. This thinking about thinking, or metacognition, helps students transfer one experience or set of skills into other situations and problems.

Students can concretize metacognition in several ways. They can write learning journals about their efforts. They can think out loud, and share their findings and frustrations. They can construct timelines that show their progress and forecast their next steps. Since different students feel comfortable with different strategies, accepting a variety of reflective approaches legitimizes diverse ways of learning and solving problems. Sharing those different styles also provides all students a broader range of ways to respond to problems.

From a different angle, students can use metacognitive process to help them examine their changing attitudes and knowledge about gender issues. Here are some starting questions they might use to analyze their work:

- What have I learned about gender issues?
- How have my assumptions or perceptions changed about gender issues?
- Do I feel more comfortable thinking and dealing with gender issues?
- Do I value other people's perspectives more?
- Do I feel more comfortable working with either sex than before?
- Do I feel more skilled working with either sex than before?
- How have I expanded my repertoire of information skills?
- How can I apply my knowledge about gender issues to my personal life?

The important point is that students become aware, both intellectually and emotionally, of their efforts and their attitudes. They can then consciously plan and regulate their work and broaden their perspectives. By continuous self-assessment, students become more responsible for and gain more control of their learning. It has more meaning, and thus becomes more powerful. It also fosters the skills needed to solve gender-sensitive problems in the real world.

Chapter 6

Designing Gender-Equitable Learning Experiences

It is not fair to ask of others what you are not willing to do yourself. —Eleanor Roosevelt

GETTING STARTED

The primary goal of any lesson is student empowerment. But it should not occur like an oasis in the desert. Rather the context of that empowerment should be a gender-equitable learning community: a safe and nurturing environment that encourages risk-taking and sharing, a weaving of independence and interdependence. All educators have the responsibility to foster that kind of learning environment within their province, be it a self-contained classroom or the library media center.

WARM-UP EXERCISES

The following activities help students become more aware of gender issues on a personal basis, and help them broaden their perspectives as they encounter gender-sensitive topics.

(1) Have males and females list the positives and negatives of being male and female. Have them compare attitudes.

(2) Have females and males assume the body postures they associate with the opposite sex. Have them discuss how they feel about their own gestures, and how they react to the body language that they see.

(3) Have students cut out faces and bodies of their own gender and their counterparts. Have them share their findings and reflections.

(4) Have students list their stresses. Have them compare them to see how many of those stresses are gender-linked.

(5) Have students compare likes and dislikes, and analyze how gender-linked those preferences are.

(6) Have students graph how they spend their time, and have them compare the results in terms of boys and girls.

(7) Have females and males act out gender role-reversals for several situations: athletic teams, weddings, birth, job promotions and transfers. Have them process their feelings and attitudes.

(8) Have students generate sex-linked words, such as "bitch," "stud," "old maid," "wolf." Have students evaluate the words in terms of connotations and status.

(9) Have students conduct content analyses of nursery rhymes and folk tales in terms of gender issues.

(10) Have students conduct content analyses of magazine and television advertisements and articles/shows.

(11) Have students write their own obituaries, and have the opposite sex analyze the obituaries in terms of gender expectations.

(12) Have students generate career decisions based on findings about each sex. For example, men are more violent so should not hold public office, especially in the military; men have more heart attacks so shouldn't be hired for stressful positions such as airline pilot. (This counteracts the statements about women not being capable because they get pregnant or have pre-menstrual syndromes.)

CONTENT

What are students learning? The short answer is curriculum; the more complex answer is skills for living. Education can be considered as abstracted and distilled experience, a way to pass on the societal wisdom without having to suffer the very real consequences of direct experience. For if one learns what the word "hot" means, s/he may never have to suffer burns. Over generations of schooling the tie with the elemental reason for education can get lost, although students remind teachers daily of that realistic need for meaning: "Why do we have to learn this?"

Looking at gender issues in education re-ignites that burning question: "What is the meaning of learning?" Thus, every content area should be embedded in life meaning. As a subject is introduced, teachers should ask themselves, "How will this information help students deal with life?" Will it provide a context for attaining skills that will help them later? Will it provide ways to examine their surroundings and make informed decisions? Will it help them understand and appreciate themselves and others better? In adult education a basic tenet for learning is: "Go from the known to the unknown." For youth, content should start with personal experience (both intellectual and emotional) and expand to embrace more generalized content. Students can then integrate and internalize content as well as give it personal meaning for their future reference. True, students can transfer abstractions to their lives, but the most authentic learning is that which most closely approximates real life, so personalizing content makes good educational sense — and it engages the students more fully. Cross-disciplinary courses begin to make that link to the real world where academic boundaries no longer apply.

In terms of gender equity, content must have personal meaning for females as well as for males. Women role models and women's approaches to life must be represented in content to have educational meaning for young women. Again, the more closely females can identify with the content at hand, the most easily they will learn, and the more profoundly they will connect with the material. Gender issues should be addressed consciously; it is not enough to subtly incorporate them into the curriculum. Otherwise, students will not develop the consciousness needed to overcome present social inequities. In fact, in some cases compensatory measures may be in order to rebalance gender opportunities. Thus, some schools offer single-sex science classes to encourage female leadership in this important subject.

RESOURCES

Since most teaching is concept-based, the stimuli for learning should be rich in variety and approach to reflect the spectrum of human experience. Thus, the textbook should be considered a launching pad for learning, not the sole vehicle of knowledge.

Assuming that textbooks are the first taste of content-related learning, teachers and students should examine them for gender sensitivity. Sex-biased materials distort reality, while sex-equitable texts expand sex rule attitudes and behavior as well as increase student motivation and comprehension (Klein, p. 219). The following aspects can guide students as they conduct content analysis of their texts, although the class can brainstorm other factors:

- Language: use of pronouns and titles
- Content: percentage of text devoted to males vs. females; status of genders portrayed
- Perspective: variety of approaches, contextual information
- Illustration: variety of males and females in terms of appearance, roles, settings, status
- Authoring: expertise by gender

Especially if a textbook lacks gender awareness, students can note the need for other resources to provide a more well-rounded perspective on content. The library should be seen as a golden opportunity for gender-equitable content as it provides different ways to examine and connect with content. Of course, the library media teacher has a special responsibility to provide those varied approaches to topics of learning by acquiring a rich collection of materials for students to use. Resources should reflect different ways of learning as well as different perspectives on information. Selection policies should be established to insure a balanced collection.

One significant goal in resource-rich learning is to provide an immediate source of self-identification for the student. But the equally important goal is to expand that experience by providing a previously unknown perspective. Thus, girls can be exposed to women's diaries about the West as a way to connect with the pioneer experience, and boys can be equally exposed to those diaries to introduce them to a *new* way of looking at the westward movement. The ultimate goal is to provide a variety of sources and a variety of ways to connect with them.

RELATING TO THE CONTENT

Assuming content is in place and resources are available to convey content in meaningful ways, the next issue is to provide a variety of ways to relate to the ideas expressed. Students need to make content their own, optimally on a visceral level. Otherwise, they may respond to it with a "so what" attitude.

Regardless of the subject, students need to get "hooked." The information must first command their attention and then involve them. For many students that requires a kinesthetic connection: playing a game, moving around the room, simulating a situation. Others must move from personal and concrete experience before they can understand abstract concepts. Particularly with early adolescent students, content should bypass the brain and speak to the students' "guts."

The easiest way for students to relate to the content is for them to apply it to their own lives: concretely and viscerally. Are they having a problem for which the content, or method of learning about the content, can be used to solve the conflict? Will learning the content make them more powerful, popular, happier, or self-confident? The closer that the content simulates reality, the easier it is for students to learn and use it.

The next most concrete way to relate to the content is by looking at the *skills* used in learning about it. For example, techniques used in comparison shopping can be transferred for comparing information sources.

Content analysis skills learned when comparing advertisements can be used to examine a friendship.

Another way to relate to the content is through *identification*. Students may imagine the hardships of pioneer life. They may identify with animal mating patterns. They might imagine visiting Paris in their foreign language class. They may feel the angst of Jane Eyre. That emotional connection facilitates learning and teaches tolerance and empathy for others.

Students should have the opportunity to reflect on the content and their relationship to it. This approach helps them relate to the ideas and internalize them holistically. It also makes them aware of their learning patterns and the ways in which they construct a meaningful body of knowledge.

The other side of reflection is sharing. Students should have ample opportunity to explore content and refine their information skills by working with others collaboratively. This approach reinforces the idea of multiple perspectives and presents a richer picture of a subject. While this book does not pretend to cover the principles of cooperative learning, the following aspects of small group work should be considered as teachers design ways for students to relate to content and to each other:

- assignment of both an academic and a social task
- assignment of students to small, heterogeneous groups
- group structure and autonomy
- small group interdependence and distributed leadership
- group and individual accountability
- processing.

EMPOWERING EXPERIENCES

Once students have the content and the knowledge, they should feel empowered; they need to feel that they can make a difference in their own lives or others' lives. They can take control. For that reason, the culminating or synthesizing experience in a unit should be meaning-rich and life-context embedded. The outcome should transcend the assignment and connect with some part of the students' lives.

For learning to be authentic, learners must validate the knowledge gained by meaningful and reflective action. Therefore, the classroom process and the product must be designed with a built-in call to real action so that students can demonstrate the fruition of their learning experience by an act of empowerment with real consequences. Because it is their show, they should plan, implement, and evaluate this final experience and, hopefully, say at the end, "We made a difference."

PLANNING AS PROCESS

As classroom and librarian teachers design and facilitate the learning environment, they model the kind of behavior that they want from their students. Their own planning should act as a mega-lesson process. The main difference between the lesson designs and the planning process is the level at which planners discuss the lesson points. In both cases, though, a main consideration is clarity; all parties must know what is going on. Let's look at a generic situation:

Scenario

One teacher looks at her/his classroom of students, and discovers how gender is affecting perception or behavior. Maybe girls aren't doing enough risk-taking; perhaps boys are condescending towards girls; probably more male than female role models are being presented in the textbook. The librarian notices that boys use the media center's computers more; the two genders approach research differently and handle frustration differently, to the detriment of the girls. The two teachers want to change the students' behaviors by addressing gender issues. On a more general basis, lessons or activities should be built on the teachers' assessment of student needs and, as much as possible, the students' own self-assessment of needs and desired outcomes.

Content Skills

The content arena is usually the responsibility of the classroom teacher, particularly in high schools that are department or content driven. The teacher looks at what the students should be able to do, and what they know — and don't know — at this point in order to achieve the specific action. Prerequisite knowledge should be ascertained so all students can start on a somewhat equitable playing field. Teachers should be cognizant of possible gender-sensitive content. Can both girls and boys relate to the topic? What prior experiences do they bring to the subject? Are gender stereotypes reinforced, such as "motherly instincts" or "manly arts"? Are gender differences acknowledged, such as dating expectations or attitudes towards violence?

Information Skills

Library teachers, as experts in resources and information literacy, typically identify these competencies and prerequisite skills. Usually the content and desired outcome determine the needed information skills. In that respect, the library teacher ordinarily reacts to the assignment rather than initiating the planning dialogue. Librarians need to talk with teachers to determine at what level students are performing relative to information skills. For instance, if the information skill entails locating and comparing two magazine articles, do students know how to use magazine indexes? If not, the assignment may need to be changed or modified. Librarians also need to be sensitive to possible gender inequities relative to information skills; for instance, boys may be more comfortable with using computers for Internet searching because they may have had more experience taking risks with remote online databases. In this example, a separate training session might be given to get all students up to speed in computer use.

Rationale for the Activity

In planning, teachers transcend the students' daily behavior and look at the long-term ramifications of the content and information processing skills to be learned. What will capture their interest? Why should students learn this? How will this activity empower them? How can the knowledge gained improve their lives or those they touch? How can gender equity be fostered through this activity?

Structure

Grade Level: The two teachers need to make sure that the skills are appropriate to the students' age or readiness. Do the students have the prerequisite skills or experiences to master the activity? Both teachers need to know.

Time Frame: Both the content skills and the information skills require time to assimilate, so the total time allotment must be negotiated. In some cases, students will work in the library media center, assess their progress in the classroom, and return to the library media center to process information at a more sophisticated level.

Resources: Here the librarian typically guides the process. In fact, the classroom teacher benefits by examining available resources and shaping the lesson to accommodate local resources (both in the school and within the community) rather than design an activity that frustrates the students' research efforts.

Grouping: Because the classroom teacher sees the students daily, s/he usually determines the group/team arrangement. However, different information skills may call for different ways to divide the assignment, which the library teacher can help determine. Work may be divided along several lines:

* individually
* pairs (same-gender, cross-gender, cross-ability)
* triads (same-gender, cross-gender, cross-ability)
* small groups of 4 to 6 members (heterogeneous gender and ability, geographic spread or homogeneity)
* jigsaw (one heterogeneous group for one task; one representative from each group to form a second group to cross-fertilize expertise on a topic)
* half class (e.g., to take one side of a debate)
* whole class (e.g., for brainstorming)

Other issues: On the teaching level, additional issues must be negotiated between the two teachers: where the activity will occur, who will teach what, where students will get help or clarification.

Activities

Working backwards from the desired behavior outcome, with the attainment of specified content and information skills to accomplish that outcome, the two teachers design activities that enable students to learn and practice the necessary competencies. Process is as important as product, so students should learn how to approach a problem as well as look at the goal. Activities should engage the students on several levels: intellectual, emotional/ psychological, and social. Students should have some say in the strategies used to attain the desired outcome; they should practice enabling behaviors that allow them control of their learning.

If students experience great frustration or don't seem to connect with the materials, teachers should be prepared to diagnose the students' prior experience and design specific, smaller-scale activities that address the students' needs. The use of small heterogeneous groups also facilitates student learning because students can build on their individual strengths and help their peers with personally more challenging skills; burdens are shared.

In some cases, learning styles should be considered. Teachers should incorporate a variety of approaches to learning to accommodate individual needs. Providing opportunities to learn through different senses and different personal interactions expands the students' repertoire of learning/coping skills and reinforces recognition of individual strengths.

Community Outreach

Both teachers can contribute their personal knowledge about the community at large. By sharing their personal networks, classroom and library teachers open up to each other and reveal their "other lives" to their students. Both students and teachers may also find that they have interests in common that they would not otherwise know about. This aspect of learning shows that all people, teachers and students, are members of a larger social group than the school. Community outreach reinforces the use of education: to live productively and fully. It also provides the linkage from school to the real world, both in terms of meaningful content and substantive action.

In terms of the specific lessons, community members provide local expertise on gender issues and offer a reality check on school-originated projects. Teachers can encourage students to interview these important citizens — and emphasize the legitimacy of oral resources. Teachers can also include community members at the evaluation stage. Community members and their agencies or institutions can help students develop and share projects to reach a broader audience more effectively by providing expertise and resources.

Who can develop lists of community resources? The first approach should be to ask the students themselves; they may do volunteer or paid work within the community, or have contacts with those who do. Classroom and library teachers have good community networks. Within the school may be structures that have connections with networks such as a career and college center, parent association, activities group, and school-to-work councils. Ideally, students should contact these groups so they have a sense of control in their learning.

Culminating Experience

This aspect of the lesson ties directly to the initial scenario. Out of student needs comes the desired outcome: the means to demonstrate learned empowerment. As much as possible, the culminating experience should relate to the outside world and to life-long learning and coping. As such, it transcends classroom and library media center, both of which are rather abstract learning environments. As much as possible, the preparation activities and resources should lay the groundwork for student-based planning and action. At this point, teachers act more as coaches and cheerleaders rather than as fonts of knowledge or directors. Probably the best analogy is a drama production; the drama teacher helps students learn the different aspects of producing a good show (e.g., acting, stagecraft, directing) and then lets the students do their own production.

The culminating experience should somehow connect the classroom experience with others. It may be a classwide exposure to real-life responses to the gender issue. It may be a student-initiated panel discussion for peers or other audiences. It may be a publication to be distributed within school or to the community.

Assessment and Evaluation

Basically, assessment measures the status of student performance. It also provides information to help plot the direction and pace of future learning. Assessment should be designed by the classroom teacher and librarian from the beginning, based on the outcome behaviors that they expect the students to exhibit. All along the way the needs, skills, activities, culminating experience, *and evaluation/assessment* should be aligned. Students should participate in the evaluation process, assessing their peers and themselves in terms of process and product. The activity of processing should empower them in this area as well as that of the experience itself since reflection and modification are marks of maturation and power.

For assessment to be authentic, it should mirror the circumstances in which students are expected to perform the skills learned. It should be as realistic as possible and as multi-faceted as the real world conditions. Several measures should be included: observation, portfolio or other documentation collection, group work, self-reflection, to name a few.

On a different level, the librarian and classroom teacher need to assess their own plans and implementation of those plans. Did what the students exhibit reflect the teachers' expectations? If not, why? While it is a very self-revealing and vulnerable activity, teacher sharing of this level of evaluation with the students is a very authentic and valuable experience for the students. Some of the guiding questions include:

- What was the balance of responsibility?
- How effective was the planning process?
- To what level did the partners support each other?
- What helped and what hindered positive results?
- How did the results affect the partnership?

Chapter 7

Lesson Plans

FRAMEWORK

The following is a key to the structures of all the lesson plans in the book. Many of the plans can be adapted to other life skills.

Scenario

This provides the contextual situation, and asks questions about it to stimulate student interest and focus attention on major themes.

Content Skills

A list is given of subjects that the students will explore.

Information Skills

Skills related to information processing are listed here. Most activities combine six major skills: task definition, information seeking strategies, location and access, use of information, synthesis, and evaluation.

Rationale for the Activity

This section answers the question, "Why are we doing this?" Gender issues are highlighted here.

Structure (several parts)

Grade Level: The general academic level for which the lesson is planned. Material can usually be modified to meet the needs of a particular set of students.

Time Frame: A guideline for predicting the amount of time required to accomplish the tasks. A class period of 45 to 60 minutes is assumed.

Approach: The focus of the lesson: either on gender as a content issue, or on the process to facilitate inclusiveness.

Resources: A general list of the types of sources that students will use to complete the tasks. In some cases, specific titles are suggested.

Grouping: Arrangement of students that will maximize the diversity of the class. In most cases, students will work in small coed groups of three to six members each.

Activities

These are the specific series of tasks that the class explores, either independently or in groups. Usually, a class discussion about the issues and information strategies sets the stage for small group exploration and research.

Community Outreach

A list is given here of local people and settings that might represent practical applications of the lesson's content. These people should be considered resources for students to interview. They also constitute the realistic context of the "culminating experience" (the next section).

Culminating Experience

The students should have a real-life (or simulated) experience that links their findings and plans with the community. In several cases a student steering committee plans the community event. While whole-class synthesis is the intent of most culminating experiences, small groups and individuals can pursue these "calls to action."

Evaluation

Both the results/plan/project and the process are evaluated for each task. In most cases groups have the opportunity for cross-evaluation among peers on these two levels. In addition, the class culminating experience (and the steering committee in some cases) is evaluated in terms of the content and information skills. For each lesson the teacher(s) and students should process their experience to synthesize their learning and extend the experience beyond the class structure. Community members should also be encouraged to evaluate the content and process as well.

BASIC LESSON PLAN FORMAT

Here is the basic format for your own lesson planning. You may modify an existing plan, or cooperatively design an original one. Empower your students!

LESSON TITLE: _____

Scenario: _____
_____

Content Skills:_____
_____

Information Skills:_____
_____

Rationale for the Activity:_____
_____

Structure: _____
_____

*Grade Level:*_____
_____

Time Frame: _____
_____

Resources: _____
_____

*Grouping:*_____
_____

Activities: _____
_____

Community Outreach: _____
_____

Culminating Experience:_____
_____

Evaluation: _____
_____

FIGHTING ABUSE

He is a good husband; he only hits me once a week.
— Wife of a Nobel Prize winner

Scenario

A friend of yours is suiting up for gym. You see bruises on an arm and a leg. "It was an accident," the friend mumbles. Monday morning your friend is dressed in long sleeves and refuses to suit up, saying that it was a rough party weekend. But you know that isn't true. You also know that no one is ever invited to your friend's house, including you. "What's going on?" you finally say as you confront your friend's behavior. The answer is, "Nothing. None of your business. And don't tell anyone." What do you do?

How many girls stay in a relationship where the boyfriend is abusive? How many children, particularly girls, are molested by family members? How often are boys *or* girls beaten up by their families? How often does emotional and psychological abuse cause family tragedy? How often do you see children who are neglected by their families? Even sadder is the knowledge that abuse continues from generation to generation. Laws permitting domestic abuse date back to Roman times:

• Romulus, a founder of Rome, suggested in his "laws of marriage" that husbands rule their wives as necessary and inseparable possessions.

• William Blackstone wrote in his *Commentaries on the Laws of England* (1760s) that "for as the husband is to answer for her misbehavior, the law thought it reasonable to intrust him with the power of chastisement."

• In 1866 a North Carolina court gave a man the right to beat his wife "with a stick as large as his finger but not larger than his thumb."

What causes relational abuse? How can you save yourself from being abused? How can the chain of relational abuse be broken?

Content Skills

• psychology and sociology of relational abuse
• safety knowledge
• recognizing and preventing relational abuse

Information Skills

• location skills
• determining correlational and cause-effect relations
• transforming information into flowchart form

Rationale for the Activity

Over one million children are abused each year in all kinds of families and relationships. Sadly, the abuser is often a person who cares for the child. Additionally, females are much more likely to be abused than males. Abuse may be physical, sexual, or emotional/psychological, or it may be manifested as neglect. This activity alerts students to the problems of abuse: its causes and effects, including gender issues. It also helps students develop ways to prevent or deal with abusive relationships.

Structure

Grade Level: middle and high school
Time Frame: 5–7 periods
Approach: focus on gender differential
Resources: materials on domestic abuse and violence, date rape and other relationship-based abuse; flowchart information. A good reference source is:

> McCue, Margi Laird. *Domestic Violence: A Reference Handbook.* Santa Barbara, CA: ABC-CLIO, 1995.

Grouping: Arrange small heterogeneous groups by types of abuse.

Activities

(1) Large-group warm-up questions (one or two students take group notes for everyone to see):

Have you seen anything on television that looked like domestic abuse? Describe it.

Have you heard in the news about any incidents of domestic abuse? Describe them.

What made those situations examples of domestic abuse: what kinds of actions took place? What kinds of words were said? How did the people look?

What kind of people do you think abuse family members?

What kind of people do you think get abused?

What are ways that family members might abuse one another?

Now, how would you define domestic abuse?

Have you heard of teens being abused by their dates or steadies? Describe a typical incident.

What patterns of behaviors do you think lead to these abusive relationships?

What kinds of people do you think get involved in abusive relationships?

Now, how would you define relationship-based abuse?
How do domestic and relationship-based abuse compare?

(2) In a large-group discussion students share their definitions and responses
to the warm-up questions about relational abuse. The class then compares the viewpoints of males and females, and analyzes why differences
occur — or don't occur. Provide dictionary definitions, and get student
reactions to the definitions. Students classify the types of abuse into the
following categories: physical, sexual, emotional/psychological, and
neglect.

(3) Taking one example of abuse, the class develops a flowchart that diagrams each of the following aspects of the abuse:
   • perpetrators and victims
   • description of abuse
   • symptoms of abuse
   • consequences of abuse (including legal)
   • prevention of abuse
   • dealing with abuse
   • gender issues
The flowchart illustrates how each step involves choice and consequences of decisions. (Students may need review in flowcharting techniques.)

(4) The class is divided into small cooperative working groups. Each group
chooses one type of abuse (e.g., sexual, neglect, etc.), and gathers information about the above aspects for that abuse. Using that data, each
group produces a detailed flowchart about the abuse. Parts of the flowchart may be documented with statistical data.

(5) Groups share their flowcharts, comparing their findings. They should
determine what patterns, if any, exist across charts. Based on their findings, the class brainstorms ways to prevent relational abuse locally.

Community Outreach

Students can gather information from the community about relational
abuse through interviews, agency publications, and local mass media. Students may brainstorm a list of feasible local experts, such as:
   • hospitals and doctors
   • public health agencies
   • women's groups
   • child advocacy groups
   • police
   • psychologists and psychiatrists

Culminating Experience

One representative from each group invites an expert in the field to talk with the class about the subject and review the groups' flowcharts.

Students can produce prevention videos or brochures for other students about relational abuse.

Evaluation

Groups cross-evaluate the flowcharts in terms of accuracy, feasibility, and thoroughness.

Groups cross-evaluate the prevention products in terms of accuracy, feasibility, and effectiveness. Local experts and outside peers can also evaluate the student products using the same criteria.

If follow-up time is allowed, those students having received the brochures or seen the video can be surveyed to see if their attitudes or behaviors changed as a result of those products.

ACROSS THE AGES

Old age is like a plane flying through a storm. Once you're aboard, there's nothing you can do. — Golda Meir

Scenario

Your club has decided to visit a nursing home as a community service. You feel uncomfortable about it because you don't know what to say to strangers, especially elderly ones. You remember the old man who sat next to you on the bus; he was smelly and he spit as he talked. You remember your grandmother who visits once a year and talks about the good old times. Your parents says she's getting senile, and they're deciding if she has to go into an old folks' home. All of these images go through your head. What should you do?

"Sure, I like getting old. Look at the alternative!" "You work like a horse, and what do you get? Old." For some people, aging is a joy; for others, it's a tedious job. In general, it's a condition experienced for a longer time by women than by men (who tend to die younger). And there's the rest of the population. How do others behave towards older people; does gender affect treatment? How do youth respond to the aged? Are old people to be shunned or consulted? Maybe there's more alike than different between teenagers and senior citizens; both can be considered marginal in the society. The joining of these two generations can accomplish something meaningful and inspiring.

Content Skills

* psychology, physiology and sociology of adolescents and senior citizens
* program development and evaluation

Information Skills

* location skills
* content analysis skills
* needs assessment techniques
* determining main ideas
* distinguishing fact from opinion

Rationale for the Activity

Senior citizens have a wealth of experience to pass on, and a surplus of time with which to do it. Young people have the energy and fresh outlook to transform the insights of older people into viable programs. In addition, both adolescents and aged are marginalized in society; their union provides strength to make a difference. When intergenerational programs are established and carried out competently, not only do young people gather valuable experience, but older people increase their productivity and self-esteem.

This activity identifies the skills of each generation, examines the reasons for possible disenfranchisement (especially for women), and works to facilitate the use of those skills in a broader constituency.

Structure

Grade Level: high school
Time Frame: 6-8 periods
Approach: working towards inclusiveness
Resources: materials on aging, adolescence, and program development. A couple of good resources include:
   Alexander, Jo. *Women and Aging.* New York: Calyx Books, 1986.
   Martz, Sandra Heldeman, ed. *If I Had My Life to Live Over I Would Pick More Daisies.* Watsonville, CA: Papier-Mache Press, 1992.
Grouping: Arrange small heterogeneous groups by kind of service project.

Activities

(1) Large-group warm-up questions (one or two students take group notes for everyone to see):

What is your image of an older person?

At what age do you consider people to be aged?

What contact do you have with older persons?

How do you feel around older persons? Why?

What problems do you think older persons might have to deal with?

What contributions do you think older persons might be able to make?

How do you think older persons are treated? Why?

What differences do you think exist between older men and older women? Why?

Do you look forward to becoming an older person? Why?

What do you think you have in common with older persons?

(2) In a large group discussion students describe their images of older people and other responses to the warm-up questions about older persons. A response grid is constructed to record thoughts according to four "cells":

Student speaker	Aged Females	Aged Males
Female	response	response
Male	response	response

The class then compares the viewpoints along gender lines. Next they identify the contributions that each age group can make. Finally, they identify commonalities between the two age groups. They also posit reasons for stereotypical societal responses, both in terms of age and gender.

(3) The class categorizes factors that possibly affect older persons; a typical list of choices would include: physiological changes, emotional changes, intellectual changes, agencies that work with older citizens, sexuality issues, housing issues, social issues. The class is divided into small cooperative working groups. Each group gathers facts about one aspect of older people. To help them structure their findings, the following framework can be used:
- Title of issue
- Description of issue
- How older persons are affected
- How gender affects the issue
- What older persons can do about the issue
- What is beyond the older person's control
- What teenagers can do about the issue

(4) Groups share their findings, and the class develops general implications.

(5) Each group develops one plan for a possible intergenerational activity. The plan should include the following variables:
   • objectives
   • abilities of the senior citizens and the adolescents
   • activities to be performed
   • demands of the site and potential "audience"
   • time frame
   • transportation
   • training
   • finances
   • permissions and other legal procedures
   • recognitions
   • gender issues

Sample intergenerational activities include: computer training, grandparenting, storytelling, crafts, oral history, writing, music.

Community Outreach

Students can gather information from the community about older persons through interviews, agency publications, and local mass media. Students may brainstorm a list of feasible local experts, such as:
   • senior citizens' groups
   • hospitals
   • health professionals
   • youth groups

Culminating Experience

The class initiates as least one intergenerational exchange. The choice of project can be based on the feasibility of each group's plan. Senior citizen advocate representatives can review the plans and talk about issues surrounding intergenerational activities. Emphasis should be put on gender issues and collaboration with older persons.

Evaluation

Groups cross-evaluate the issues framework for their sources of information, accuracy, thoroughness, and quality of presentation.

Groups cross-evaluate intergenerational activity plans according to the criteria used to gather information. Local experts and older persons evaluate the intergenerational activity in terms of its planning and implementation (e.g., did the participants learn from each other, did everyone feel included and valued, did participants feel comfortable and did they enjoy themselves?).

CARE AND NURTURING OF ANIMALS

Animals were once, for all of us, teachers. They instructed us in ways of being, and perceiving that extended our imaginations that were models for additional possibilities.
— Joan McIntyre

Scenario

The issue of raising kids has come up in dating conversation. Each person thinks the other should shoulder major responsibility for the job. "Look at how mother animals always take care of their young," the guy says. "Remember when you got a puppy? You spent all your free time with it," counters the female. "Listen, let's not worry about it. Kids are a long way off, and when the time comes it'll work itself out just fine." Or will it? What do you do?

Is the parenting role gender-linked? Is it dictated by society or is it instinctive? Do gender roles differ for other animals? What are factors to think about when raising children that might involve gender roles? What are workable options for people?

Content Skills

• male and female roles in birthing and care of offspring for different animals
• development patterns (growth and time frames) of animals
• biological knowledge related to animals

Information Skills

• location skills
• classification skills
• sequencing skills

- analyzing information to determine relationships
- transforming data into chart form
- developing and testing working hypotheses

Rationale for the Activity

Gender roles are hotly debated when it comes to raising children. Examining gender roles across species provides a theoretical basis upon which to compare human practices and test existing myths about nurturing roles. By examining the needs of offspring and the influence of gender in raising them, students can make more effective decisions about child-rearing.

Structure

Grade Level: high school
Time Frame: 8-12 periods
Approach: working towards inclusiveness
Resources: animal and child-rearing resources, people and other animal caregivers, database computer software if a database or spreadsheet is generated
Grouping: Arrange small heterogeneous groups by species.

Activities

(1) Large-group warm-up questions (one or two students take group notes for everyone to see):

Note: Teachers need to be sensitive to the variations in family makeup. Less than 10% of today's families consist of the traditional bread-winning father, homemaker wife, together with their biological children. Some students may feel uncomfortable about sharing their family situation, so they should be assured that they can speak from their experiences with their extended family, their relatives, or other families that they know.

What is the role of the family in raising children?

Who is in charge of raising children in your family?

What is the male's role in raising children in your (extended) family?

What is the female's role in raising children in your (extended) family?

On television and film what child-rearing roles do males and females assume?

What do you think are the expected roles of males and females in raising children?

What do you think determines which gender takes responsibility for raising children?

Do you think it matters what roles males and females have in raising children? Why?

(2) The class generates a two-column list (Fathers vs. Mothers) of existing myths and assumptions about gender roles in child-rearing, such as "Mothers should nurture; fathers should discipline." Note the brainstormers' genders beside their statements. The class surveys their existing stances on those myths.

An important issue needs to be addressed: that of social structure and support systems. Economic issues, employment issues, family structure, presence of extended families, availability of child care, even neighborhood support systems influence the decision on how children are raised. If time allows, students can rank the relative importance of these issues in determining gender responsibilities.

(2a) If time allows, the class can be divided into two groups: male role and female role. The two groups research the validity of the statements made in the class brainstorm session.

(3) The class generates a list of tasks in child-rearing, such as: pre-natal care, health issues, safety issues, monitoring growth and development, skills to be taught, socialization, gender issues, etc. A small group follows up on the list by researching other possible tasks. They report back to the class, modifying the list.

(3a) If time allows, the class can rank the relative importance of child-rearing tasks. Male and female rankings can be kept separate, then cross-analyzed for patterns and discrepancies.

(4) To further highlight gender perceptions, the child-rearing list of factors are examined in terms of each gender's degree of responsibility. The following structure facilitates comparisons:

FEMALE'S RESPONSIBILITY	TASK	MALE'S RESPONSIBILITY
....	Feeding	....
....	Getting inoculations	....

Students place an X along the spectrum to indicate who is responsible for the task. As a whole, the class generated a chart that shows the range of responses for each task, and then discusses the gender role implications. The class-generated chart may look like:

FEMALE'S RESPONSIBILITY   TASK   MALE'S RESPONSIBILITY

..................XXXXXXXXXXXXX Feeding XXXXXXXX...........................
.....XXX............................. Getting inoculations ....XXX..........

Alternatively, the class can "vote by foot." One end of the room is designated "Male's total responsibility," and the other end is designated "Female's total responsibility." As each child-rearing task is called out, students put themselves on the line in terms of male-female balance of responsibility.

In either case, the class analyzes the perceptions and discusses possible reasons for arriving at certain conclusions (e.g., existing models, cultural background, religious upbringing, social support systems, personal preference, etc.). This discussion provides insights into how people develop expectations.

(5) Students test those myths against the practices of other animals by locating information about gender roles for rearing animal offspring. The class is divided into small cooperative working groups. Each group chooses a species. The issue of transferability of findings should be discussed before starting. Students may generate a list of factors that affect different child-rearing practices, such as: social structure (e.g., ant colony vs. nuclear family), life span (e.g., elephant vs. butterfly), environment (e.g., ocean), food (e.g., milk vs. worms), reproduction (e.g., mammal vs. reptile). Thus, students may elect to choose only mammalian species with social structures resembling humans' because of their relative proximity to humans.

(6) Each group generates a chart about offspring-rearing that incorporates the different tasks; gender roles should be highlighted. The class needs to come to consensus on the format of the charts so different species can be compared. One option is to choose one representative of each group to form a class task force on standardization; that task force brainstorms and chooses the presentational format, such as: charts, timelines, databases. One simple format would be to echo the chart generated in step 5 for each species.

(7) Groups are rearranged such that one representative from each research group forms a new group to compare one specific offspring-rearing task across species, such as pre-natal care. A comparison chart is made to illustrate trends.

(8) Groups report their findings, and the class verbally develops an overall stance on gender roles in child-rearing.

Community Outreach

Students can gather information from the community about gender roles in raising children through observations, interviews, agency publications, and local mass media. Students may brainstorm a list of feasible local experts, such as:

- zoos
- veterinarians
- child-care centers
- recreational centers
- pediatric doctors and hospital services

Culminating Experience

Groups visit zoos, veterinarians, hospitals, or child-care centers to observe animal and child behaviors. Groups interview experts about gender-linked practices in offspring-rearing. After gathering community information, groups share their findings with the rest of the class, and revise the class's stance on gender roles in child-rearing.

Alternatively, a steering committee organizes a class panel discussion with the above experts about gender roles in offspring-rearing.

To document their findings, groups can videotape visits (note: permission releases must be obtained when taping individuals). Alternatively, students can share their species and child-rearing tasks charts with other classes.

Evaluation

Groups cross-evaluate species-based group efforts in terms of: sources used, completeness, accuracy of conclusions, and organization of data.

At the second stage, groups cross-evaluate group analysis and interpretation of data, and conclusions.

Groups cross-evaluate the culminating experience in terms of the findings' validity and quality of presentation. Local experts also evaluate the group presentations or products using the same criteria.

The teacher and students evaluate the large group in terms of idea-generation, consensus-building, and format development.

MUSING ABOUT ART

*What was any art but a mould in which to imprison for a
moment the shining, elusive element which is life itself.*
—Willia Cather

Art is not a pastime but a priesthood. — Jean Cocteau

Scenario

There are some real mixed messages about art. Some people don't consider it a serious field, especially for men, but the majority of known artists
seem to be males. Women are portrayed more often than men, but they seem
to be considered objects rather than respected subjects. Women supposedly
inspire artists; consider the Muses. Yet women don't seem to get much credit
for their influence in the artist's real life. What gives?

Content Skills

• technical artistic skills
• knowledge about artists
• career information about art industries

Information Skills

• location skills
• content analysis skills
• visual literacy

Rationale for the Activity

The field of art interests both males and females, but gender messages
about art are sometimes confusing and contradictory. This activity explores
those gender issues, and encourages people to look at art with a broader perspective.

Structure

Grade Level: high school
Time Frame: 4-6 periods
Approach: focus on gender differential
Resources: art books. Two interesting sources are:

Betsky, Aaron. *Building Sex: Men, Women, Architecture, and the Construction of Sexuality.* New York: William Morrow, 1995.
Confessions of the Guerrilla Girls. New York: HarperCollins, 1995.
Grouping: Arrange small heterogeneous groups by art career or by historical period.

Activities

(1) Large-group warm-up questions (for all to see and to use for follow-up comparisons, one student records boys' statements and one student records girls' statements):

Do you think of art as a masculine or a feminine subject? Why?

Why do you think there are more known male artists than female ones?

Do you think the subject of a piece of work makes it more or less significant? Why?

What kinds of art subjects do you think should be taken seriously? Why?

Do you think certain types of art are more serious than others? If so, what?

Do you consider jewelry to be a serious art form? Why?

Do you consider quilts to be a serious art form? Why?

The class analyzes their responses, and discusses the basis for their opinions.

(2) The class divides into two halves. One half examines gender issues in art from the point of view of the subject matter. Within each half, small heterogeneous working groups are formed. Each group compares how males and females are portrayed in art during a specific art movement (e.g., Impressionism, Baroque, Dadaism). To structure their content analysis, this half of the class brainstorms criteria for evaluation. Factors may include:
- setting
- person's body language
- role of the figure
- dress/undress
- message or theme
- artistic technique: color, shading, use of line, etc.

(3) The other half of the class examines gender issues in art from the point of view of artistic careers. Each small group examines the roles of males and females within a specific field (e.g., advertising, computer-aided design, fashion, industrial design, interior decoration, teaching, set design). To

structure their content analysis, this half of the class brainstorms criteria for evaluation. Factors may include:

- number of people in the field
- proportion of females to males
- job descriptions
- salary range
- job security
- opportunities for advancement
- educational requirements

(4) Each half of the class shares their findings among their groups, and draws conclusions from their evidence. Then the two halves share their conclusions (backed by the evidence) with each other.

Community Outreach

Students gather community information about art. They may attend art shows, conduct interviews, and examine local coverage. Students may brainstorm a list of feasible art experts, such as:

- art instructors
- professional artists
- local art groups and organizations

Culminating Experience

The class as a whole, or by groups, develops and implements a play to showcase women artists. They may create a video, plan an exhibit, produce a traveling slide show, write articles for local publications, or hold an artists' fair.

Evaluation

Groups cross-evaluate the content analyses in terms of accuracy, thoroughness, quality of evidence, and presentation.

Local experts, participants, and the teacher evaluate the final projects in terms of planning (was it feasible and well developed?), implementation (quality of content, appropriateness of presentation, technical quality), and impact on the community.

AWARD-WINNING WOMEN

Fame is a pearl many dive for and only a few bring up.
— Louisa May Alcott

Scenario

You read the lists of Nobel Prize winners, and they tend to be men. Is this the case for other awards, such as Pulitzers and Grammys? What kinds of awards do women win? What awards are limited to women? How are awards selected? Who chooses the winners? What can you do to change the situation relative to awards for women?

Content Skills

- identification of different awards
- knowledge of awards criterion

Information Skills

- location skills
- content analysis skills
- knowledge of specialized references

Rationale for the Activity

Awards reveal social values and validate certain human achievements. Women are underrepresented in many award fields. In those areas where women excel, awards are largely absent. This activity encourages students to examine the basis for honoring achievement and selecting winners, and to explore the reasons that certain groups are underrepresented. It also challenges students to consider ways to alter the situation, such as: changing criterion, changing judges, creating awards, or facilitating the work situation to encourage women's achievements.

Structure

Grade Level: high school
Time Frame: 5-6 periods
Approach: focus on gender differential
Resources: specialized references on awards, biographies, selection procedures. A good source is:

Opfell, Olga S. *The Lady Laureates: Women Who Have Won the Nobel Prize.* 2nd ed. Metuchen, NJ: Scarecrow Press, 1986.
Grouping: Arrange small heterogeneous groups by award type.

Activities

(1) Large-group warm-up questions (one or two students take group notes for everyone to see):
What are some of the awards for achievement you can name?
What kinds of achievements are recognized?
What kinds of people do you think tend to be awarded?
How do you think award winners are selected?
Do you think that genders are equitably represented as award winners?

(2) The class lists possible awards. Groups are set up by award. Graphic representation of information is reviewed, and a standard format is established by consensus (or teacher directive). The typical graph is a bar graph where number of awardees is measured, male vs. female, by year.

(3) The class is divided into small cooperative working groups. Each group gathers data about one award by gender over time, and creates a graph overhead transparency to present the data visually. They also research the criterion and judge selection, if possible. Each group interprets the information, drawing a conclusion from the data.

(4) Groups report their findings and conclusions. The class compares the findings and generates general conclusions.

(5) New groups are constructed by including one representative from each original group. Each new group develops an award and writes up accompanying procedures (criterion, judge selection, nominations process). Each group selects at least one female winner for each award.

(6) Students individually choose an award that they want to attain. They develop a game plan towards that goal. In pairs, students compare plans and give suggestions to improve or facilitate the plan. A sample framework is:

GOAL:

Steps:	*Obstacles:*	*Changes Needed:*	*Deadline:*	*Accountability:*
1.				
2.				
3.				

SUPPORT SYSTEM: (who can help)

Community Outreach

Students can gather information from the community about local awards through interviews, agency publications, and local mass media. Students may brainstorm a list of feasible local experts, such as:
- local awards committees
- judges for awards
- school award committees and judges

Culminating Experience

Students stage a simulated awards ceremony in which they award women and men for their achievements. The awards should include criterion and judge selection.

Students conduct letter campaigns to alter present award procedures to provide more inclusiveness. This activity may require additional time to teach related writing skills.

Evaluation

Groups cross-evaluate group efforts in content analysis, graphic presentation, and conclusions.

At the second stage, groups cross-evaluate efforts in developing award criterion, judge selection, nominations, and awarding of achievements.

Pairs evaluate each other's plans in terms of feasibility, specificity, and thoroughness.

SETTING UP A BUSINESS

To be successful, a woman has to be better at her job than a man. —Golda Meir

Scenario

A vacant warehouse across from a city convention center is available for lease. A group of women wish to assume control of the building, using it as a co-op of privately owned businesses run by women. What actions do they have to complete in order to insure a successful venture?

What skills and attitudes are needed to start a business? How do you get the start-up money? What obstacles must be overcome? What are the changes that new businesses can make a real go — and last? What kind of support is available? In what way is gender a positive or a negative factor in starting a business? In the final analysis, is working for yourself worth all the work?

Content Skills

- business/financial competencies
- legal knowledge
- planning skills
- interpersonal skills

Information Skills

- location skills
- interviewing skills
- determining main facts
- determining cause-effect relationships

Rationale for the Activity

One of the fast-growing sectors in the economy is entrepreneurship in small business, and women dominate this field. This activity gives students an opportunity to examine the specific steps to establishing a business while becoming aware of the specific challenges and opportunities that women face in the business world. The activity also examines how business affects people's personal lives.

Structure

Grade Level: high school
Time Frame: 8-10 periods
Approach: working towards inclusiveness
Resources: business persons and organizations, business and legal sources. Good sources include:
> Bergmann, B. *The Economic Emergence of Women*. New York: Basic Books, 1988.
> Borman, Kathryn M., Daisy Quarm, and Sarah Gideonse, ed. *Women in the Workplace: Effects on Families*. Norwood, NJ: Ablex, 1984.
> Carr-Ruffino, Norma. *The Promotable Woman*. 2nd ed. Belmont, CA: Wadsworth Publishing, 1993.

Gilman, Charlotte Perkins. *Women and Economics: The Economic Factor Between Men and Women as a Function of Social Evolution.* New York: Harper & Row, 1966.

Godfrey, J. *Our Wildest Dreams: Women Entrepreneurs Making Money, Having Fun, Doing Good.* New York: Harper Business, 1992.

Larkin, Geraldine A. *Woman to Woman: Street Smarts for Women Entrepreneurs.* Englewood Cliffs, NJ: Prentice-Hall, 1993.

Grouping: This project may be grouped in two ways: by business or by organizational task. In the former method, each group selects a possible business and researches the processes needed to insure a successful venture. The latter approach examines the project on a macro level, and assigns a procedural task to each small cooperative group. Ideally, groups should be involved with an overall procedural task, then reassigned tasks according to a specific potential business.

Activities

(1) Large-group warm-up questions (one or two students take group notes for everyone to see):

Have you ever thought about starting your own business? Why?

What do you think would be the advantages of starting your own business?

What do you think would be the disadvantages of starting your own business?

What do you think would be the hardest part of starting your own business?

What skills do you think you have that would help you start a business?

What skills do you think you need to learn in order to start a business?

What kind of help would you seek in order to start a business?

Where would you go to get help in order to start a business?

Do you think men or women would have an easier time starting a business? Why?

(2) The class brainstorms the various processes leading up to a successful cooperative business venture. Points that should arise include:

• legal issues: getting permits, incorporating a business, etc.

• financial issues: buying vs. leasing property, costs for setting up a business, labor costs, grant/sponsorship sources

• site issues: use of space, convention or seasonal use

• product/service issues: marketing, staffing, space use

• communications issues: networking with other businesses, advertising, etc.

• impact on personal life

Students may need to consult business sources first in order to get ideas on how to establish a business.

(3) The class discusses what women's issues would arise:
- Is it easier for a man to be the "front?"
- Are monies available for women's businesses?
- What labor laws apply specifically to women?
- What interpersonal skills might be gender-sensitive?

(4) The class is divided into small cooperative working groups. Each group is assigned to gather data on each process or issue. They should brainstorm possible sources of information:
- print materials on business, including government publications
- interviews with community business and government people.

(5) The groups report their findings and develop an overall business plan.

(6) New groups are established, consisting of a representative from each original group. The second groups do specific data gathering on a potential specific business. They follow the steps above: researching start-up issues, noting relevant women's issues, and developing a business plan.

Community Outreach

Students gather information from the community about starting a business. They can interview experts, read agency publications, and examine local mass media. Students may brainstorm a list of feasible local experts, such as:
- local chambers of commerce
- business people and organizations
- Junior Achievement groups
- Junior Women's Leagues

Culminating Experience

A student steering committee plans a panel discussion about starting businesses, inviting local women to talk about their experiences starting businesses. If they have the class's business plans ahead of time, they can critique them, and offer suggestions at the open session.

Evaluation

Groups cross-evaluate group efforts in terms of sources used, conclusions drawn, and thoroughness of plans. Groups evaluate their ability to work together and fully participate.

If the second stage, establishing a specific business, is achieved, groups cross-evaluate findings in terms of each step: market testing, financial considerations, space allocation, hiring, legal issues, communications.

If students plan the panel discussion, they are evaluated in terms of their planning and implementation.

CAN WE TALK?

Self-expression must pass into communication for its fulfillment. — Pearl S. Buck

Scenario

"I don't get it," says one football player to another. "Last night I told Susan I'd call her later, and she yelled at me today because I didn't phone her back. Later is later, you know?" "Girls, what do you expect?" says his buddy.

"I was waiting all night. Jim left me hanging even though he said he'd phone me later." "What a jerk," says her girlfriend, "you can never trust guys." Who's in the right? *Is* there a right side? What would you do?

"Walk at one, talk at two" is a familiar saying. People learn early to communicate; in fact, the youngest baby can communicate needs well enough to make parents respond quickly. Yet adults still have troubles communicating, and speaking to the opposite sex can feel like talking to aliens. In addition, the variety of ways to communicate — and miscommunicate — can be overwhelming. And sometimes no communicating can be an effective form of communicating! How do you get your message across so others respond appropriately?

Content Skills

- verbal skills
- written skills
- visual skills
- language skills
- listening skills

Information Skills

- location skills
- content analysis skills

- classification skills
- determining correlations and cause-effect relationships
- transforming information into a variety of media

Rationale for the Activity

Communication is a daily activity, one that often gets overlooked or underanalyzed. Recently, gender issues relative to communication have taken on added significance. This activity helps students understand the communication process and explore many communication methods. The intent is for students to become more effective communicators.

Structure

Grade Level: middle and high school
Time Frame: 5-7 periods
Approach: working towards inclusiveness
Resources: communications sources; index cards. Good books on gender issues include:

Elgin, Suzette D. *Genderspeak.* New York: Wiley, 1993.
Gardner, Howard. *Frames of Mind.* New York: Basic Books, 1983.
Kroeger, Otto and Janet M. Thuessen. *Type Talk.* New York: Delacorte Press, 1988.
Reardon, Kathleen. *They Don't Get It, Do They? Communication in the Workplace — Closing the Gap Between Women and Men.* Boston: Little, Brown and Company, 1995.
Tannen, Deborah. *Gender and Discourse.* New York: Oxford University Press, 1994.
Tannen, Deborah. *You Just Don't Understand.* New York: William Morrow, 1990.

Grouping: Arrange small heterogeneous groups by communications step and afterwards by communications method.

Activities

(1) As a large-group warm-up exercise have students role-play different scenarios. Each scene can be played several ways:
- two boys act as two boys
- two boys act as two girls
- two boys act as a boy and a girl
- two girls act as two girls
- two girls act as two boys
- two girls act as a girl and a boy

- a boy and a girl act as their own gender
- a boy and a girl act as the opposite gender

Students can brainstorm scenes, such as:
- trying to convince the other person to do something risky (e.g., cheat, have intercourse, bungee-jump)
- breaking up a relationship (e.g., romantic, working)
- asking a favor (e.g., borrow money, use a car)

Ideally, both actors know which gender they are to portray, but only one person knows the issue ahead of time. Players have one minute to prepare their skit, and a maximum of three minutes to act it out.

The rest of the class observes the skit, and discusses the choice of topic, the words used to convey the message, the body language, and the outcome. To increase participation, the class can be divided into two groups so twice as many people can do role-plays.

(2) In a large group, students discuss *what* people communicate and *why* they want to communicate. Main reasons for communication typically include: to inform, to gather information, to motivate, to instruct, to persuade, to help. Each reason should be written on a separate index card, to be used in the culminating experience. Students share their perceptions about possible gender differences.

(3) In a large group, students brainstorm *ways* to communicate, and discuss the characteristics of each method of communicating. Students share their perceptions about possible gender issues. Typical methods include: writing, verbal, visual, body language, dress. Each of these means can be subdivided; e.g., written communication includes essays, poems, plays, advertisements, memos, flyers, manuals, etc.

(4) In a large group, students share their perceptions about the process of communication. Then they compare it with a formal model, such as:

PERSON »» IDEA »» EXPRESSED MEDIUM »»
COMMUNICATION CHANNEL (AND CONTEXT) »»
RECEIVER »» INTERNAL SYSTEM »» EXPRESSED RESPONSE

(5) The class is divided into small heterogeneous groups, each one researching aspects of one step in the communications process. The class may concentrate on one means of communication to help them focus on the process. To aid in comparing findings, groups should categorize their findings; this may be done as a class brainstorming session or be provided to them by the teacher. Typical categories include: description, examples, role of step, significance of step, consequences of miscommunication, possible barriers,

ways to enhance communication, gender issues. The lists of examples for each step in the communication process are copied onto index cards to be used in the culminating experience.

Note: the communications channel step should be subdivided into components: e.g., time frame, environment, location/space, culture, situation.

(6) One representative from each original group constitutes new groups, each of which focuses on one method of communication. Each group examines the communication process for their method, listing the advantages and disadvantages of their method at each step.

(7) Groups report their findings and conclusions to the rest of the class. The large group discusses possible implications.

Community Outreach

Students gather information from the community about communications. They can conduct interviews and examine local communications companies. Students may brainstorm a list of feasible local experts, such as:
- mass communications and advertising agencies
- writers
- photographers
- psychologists and sociologists

Culminating Experience

Student pairs draw one index card (activity step 5) for each step in the communications process and for the communication objective, and role-play the communications encounter while the rest of the class observes and evaluates the process. A second pair role-plays the situation using the same criteria, with the large group comparing the processes. Community communications experts can also evaluate and comment on the process.

Evaluation

Groups cross-evaluate each step of the communications process in terms of accuracy, thoroughness, and effectiveness.

Groups cross-evaluate communications methods in terms of accuracy, thoroughness, and effectiveness.

Groups and communications experts evaluate role-plays in terms of feasibility and communications effectiveness.

FEMALE-FRIENDLY COMPUTERS

If I had learned to type, I never would have made brigadier general. — Elizabeth Hoisington

Men want to force computers to submit. Women just want computers to work. — Deborah Tannen

Scenario

You decide that it's time to buy a computer, so you go to the local store. One gender is definitely in charge. Preteen boys are hogging the demonstration models. In the entertainment section war games predominate. Most of the sales clerks are males. People seem to ignore you. How do you feel? Probably, you either feel comfortable and part of the gang, or you feel like an alien, depending on whether you're male or female.

What is your relationship with computers: love/hate/avoid? What influences your attitude towards computers? What gender roles exist relative to computers? How can you establish a meaningful relationship with computers?

Content Skills

- computer literacy
- career opportunities using computers

Information Skills

- location skills
- drawing conclusions from a variety of sources
- determining correlations and cause-effect relationships
- transforming data into graphic form
- organizing and synthesizing information
- classification skills
- interviewing skills

Rationale for the Activity

Most studies indicate that females use computers less than males. Particularly since computers are seen as significant information tools, equitable access and skill should be a goal for education. A variety of factors influence computer use: personal attitudes and experience, societal attitudes, even software development, which seems to favor stereotypical male behavior. This activity encourages students to look at computer usage in terms of gender, and to develop ways to facilitate computer equity.

Structure

Grade Level: middle and high school
Time Frame: 5-10 periods
Approach: working towards inclusiveness
Resources: computer resources, hardware and software, computer experts. A good source for teachers is:
> Sanders, Jo and Mary McGinnis. *The Computer Equity Workshop Set.* Metuchen, NJ: Scarecrow Press, 1991.

Grouping: Arrange small heterogeneous groups by software title or type.

Activities

(1) Large-group warm-up questions (two students take group notes for everyone to see, one to record what girls say and one to record what boys say):
   What words come to mind when I say "computer"?
   Describe the typical computer expert.
   How do you use computers?
   What do you like about computers?
   What would you like to change about computers?

(2) Student pairs interview each other regarding their attitudes about computer learning and use. They then report their findings to the rest of the class, noting differences along gender lines. Typical interview questions can include:
   What experiences have you had with computers?
   Where do you use computers?
   How often do you use computers? Is that adequate time?
   Do you talk about computers with your peers? What do you say?
   What kinds of programs do you use?

(3) The class generates a list of computer use factors, such as: availability of computers at home, hours spent using the computer, type of computer applications used. They then conduct a class survey, separating female and male responses. The class is divided into small cooperative working groups. Each group generates a graph of one factor, and interprets the data. The class as a whole draws conclusions on the data.

(4) (Optional) The class generates a set of questions to ask at a computer store (product and technical information, pricing, assistance, hiring) and a set of factors to record when going to a computer store (e.g., gender of customers and sales persons, types of software available, degree of help and attention). Have pairs of students (single sex and mixed sex) go to computer stores, and ask the same set of questions. Students record the experience and report back to the class as the basis for a large-group discussion on social attitudes about computers and gender.

(5) The class discusses the variety of software and generates a standardized checklist of evaluation factors, such as: content, gender roles, action, interactivity, language, ease of use, transfer to real life. Small groups then evaluate a piece of software using the checklist, and report their findings (both the evaluation and the process).

(6) (Optional) Each small group chooses an area of interest, such as music or sports, and researches careers in that field which incorporate computer technology. In examining career opportunities, they should look at gender issues (e.g., background, hiring, specialties, quotas, salaries, career patterns). Each group determines how to share their information and makes a presentation to the class. (If necessary, the entire class can brainstorm ways to share information: skit, collage, flipcharts, video, slide show, etc.)

(7) Each group develops a brochure to facilitate female involvement with computers and computer use.

Community Outreach

Students gather information from the community about computers. They can conduct interviews, read agency publications, and examine local mass media. Students may brainstorm a list of feasible local experts, such as:
- local businesses that incorporate computer technology
- local computer companies
- higher education faculty and computer departments

Culminating Experience

A student steering committee invites a panel of women in computer careers to share their experiences, particularly in terms of gender issues. Small groups should develop questions ahead of time to guide the discussion. Ideally, each group should find a woman in the field, and invite/host her. A representative from each group forms the steering committee to organize the panel event. The adult panel can also review and discuss the groups' gender equity brochures.

Students can also "shadow" a person who works with computers for a living and find out what kind of preparation is needed for the job. (This can be a group video project to share with the rest of the class.)

The class can publish their computer use brochures and distribute them at school and in the community.

The class can make recommendations to computer store management about gender equity.

Evaluation

Groups cross-evaluate group effort, accuracy and thoroughness in constructing a chart and interpreting the data, examining software, and developing an equity brochure.

If research is done, groups cross-evaluate the presentations in terms of content and sharing.

The class evaluates the panel steering group in terms of planning and implementation effectiveness.

DO YOU HAVE
A CONSUMING PASSION?

In spite of the cost of living, it's still popular. — Kathleen Norris

Scenario

You just bought a new pair of tennis shoes on sale, and you're ready to hit a few balls. After the first set, though, you see the stitching coming apart. When you go back to the store to get your money back, the sales clerk refuses to exchange the shoes because you've worn them. You try to get the manager's attention. Finally, some action. But the shoe sale is over, and you're expected to pay full price if you want another pair of shoes. What should you do?

Have you ever bought a lemon? What if a new outfit rips the first time you use it? What recourse would you have if a landlord didn't make the repairs you requested? As a female, how can you be sure to get the same deal as a male on a computer? How do you build a good credit rating, and does marital status affect it? Can you sue if you have an accident in someone's home? How can you become a savvy, cost-conscious consumer who's treated fairly?

Content Skills

• consumer skills: comparison buying, contracts, credit, time-purchases, ecology, money management
  • repair skills
  • legal knowledge
  • mathematical skills
  • accounting skills

Information Skills

• location skills
• using primary documents
• interviewing skills
• determining main facts
• distinguishing fact from opinion
• organizing and transforming data onto a spreadsheet
• organizing and transforming information into flowchart form
• organizing and comparing data in bar graph form
• synthesizing information as a simulation

Rationale for the Activity

It has been said that the United States is a land of consumerism: buy, buy, buy. But not everyone has the skills to consume wisely. Furthermore, one's gender and lifestyle can make a difference relative to consumerism. This activity alerts students to the variety of consumer issues that they face already and will soon confront, and prepares them to manage personal funds.

Structure

Grade Level: high school
Time Frame: 8-10 periods
Approach: working towards inclusiveness

Resources: material on money management and consumer issues, repair manuals, legal sources, ledgers or spreadsheet computer programs
Grouping: Arrange small heterogeneous groups by consumer issue.

Activities

(1) Each student creates a hypothetical monthly budget and compares the results in pairs. In a large group students compare budgets and their consumer assumptions.

(2) The class identifies consumer issues. Typical issues include:
   • comparison buying
   • contract
   • credit and credit ratings
   • investments
   • insurance
   • legal issues: rights, suits, bankruptcy
   • banking

(3) The class is divided into small groups by consumer issue. Group members first share their present perceptions about the issue, including possible gender differences. Then they identify expert sources of information, and gather data about the issue, including sample forms and policies. Each group develops a flowchart to diagram the process associated with effective consumer practice. For each issue, impact of gender and marital status should be noted; separate data into the following groups: female, male, single, married, divorced. Comparative numerical data should be represented in bar graph form.
   Note: students may need additional time to practice interviewing and creating spreadsheets.

(4) One representative from each group constitutes a new group, who develop a year-long consumer simulation according to one gender/marital status (e.g., single female). Included in the scenario are typical situations such as check overdrafts, income changes, unexpected expenses, purchases requiring contracts or policies. Incorporate sample forms or policies whenever possible. Each group documents their financial status in ledger form, and notes how they made their consumer decisions.

(5) Groups exchange their year-long consumer simulations, and have the readers make independent decisions. The paired groups compare the two results, and report their findings to the entire class for further discussion.

Community Outreach

Students gather information from the community about consumerism. They can conduct interviews and examine local mass media. Students may brainstorm a list of feasible local experts, such as:
- financial institutions
- Better Business Bureau
- insurance representatives
- investment counselors and money managers
- legal advisors
- consumer groups

Culminating Experience

A student steering committee invites community consumer experts to act as a visiting panel. They can review and evaluate the flowcharts and simulations, or speak more globally about consumer issues. A student group can videotape the panel discussion for distribution to other students or the community.

Alternatively, students can develop consumer seminars for other students or community members.

Evaluation

Groups cross-evaluate consumer issue bar graphs and flowcharts in terms of accuracy, clarity, and thoroughness.

Groups cross-evaluate simulations in terms of feasibility, accuracy, decision-making process, and substantiation of conclusions.

Consumer experts evaluate group findings and simulations in terms of accuracy, thoroughness, and presentation quality.

IT'S A CRIME

You cannot shake hands with a clenched fist.
— Indira Gandhi

Scenario

You're on a crowded subway on your way home. It's rush hour, and you feel hot and tired and squeezed. At one point, you feel someone rub up against you. You turn around, but the person looks unaware; you try to forget it and hope it was unintentional. Then just as your stop is coming up, you feel a slight tug. As you make your way to the door, you suddenly realize that someone has snatched your wallet. A couple of kids push their way through the crowd past you, and you try to catch them. It's no use. What should you do?

Crimes are committed daily, sometimes intentionally and sometimes not. Have you ever been a victim of crime, such as theft or harassment? Have you ever committed a crime, such as underage drinking or reckless driving? What constitutes a crime? What recourse do you have if a crime is committed against you? What can you do to prevent crime?

Content Skills

- legal knowledge
- knowledge about crime and punishment

Information Skills

- location skills
- determining main facts
- determining correlations and cause-effect relationships
- categorizing skills
- organizing and synthesizing information into written and visual form

Rationale for the Activity

Crime is a much-discussed topic. Statistics report that crime is on the rise. Students, particularly women, may feel powerless in the face of such an environment. This activity enables them to gather facts about crime and crime prevention.

Structure

Grade Level: high school
Time Frame: 5-8 periods
Approach: focus on gender differential
Resources: legal and crime sources. A couple of good sources are:
  McCue, Margi Laird. *Domestic Violence: A Reference Handbook.* Santa Barbara, CA: ABC-CLIO, 1995.
  Miedzian, M. *Boys Will Be Boys: Breaking the Link Between Masculinity and Violence.* New York: Doubleday, 1991.
Grouping: Arrange small heterogeneous groups by type of crime.

Activities

(1) In a large group, students discuss crime and its impact. Students share their feelings about crime as it applies to them personally: how safe they feel, how they avoid or deal with crime, how much control they feel. Students compare the responses of males and females.

(2) Students brainstorm different kinds of criminal action. Typical crimes include: alcohol- and drug-related, fraud, financial, bodily, weapons-related, disturbances, property-related (e.g., burglary, trespassing, vandalism), harassment.

(3) The class is divided into small heterogeneous groups by type of crime. Each group researches their topic, organizing their findings into the following categories: legal description of the crime, relevant statistics about criminals and victims, consequences, recourse for victims, and preventative measures. As much as possible, students should break down their findings within each category according to the following grid:

Category	Female	Male	
Under 18			
18 and over			

(4) Four new groups are formed (one per grid cell), with representatives from each original group. Each group compares findings across crime types within their one grid cell, and draws conclusions based on the evidence gathered.

(5) Each group reports their findings to the rest of the class, and large-group conclusions are made. Students brainstorm ways to act on the findings: e.g., teach prevention measures, create laws on crime, establish counseling mechanisms, create awareness games for children.

Community Outreach

Students gather information from the community about crime. They can conduct interviews, visit correctional agencies, and read crime reports. Students may brainstorm a list of feasible local experts, such as:
- legal experts
- enforcement agencies
- penal institutions

Culminating Experience

By crime type, groups develop and implement one action plan against crime. Community crime experts can critique plans and provide guidance.

Evaluation

Groups cross-evaluate findings about crimes in terms of accuracy, thoroughness, and presentation quality.

Groups cross-evaluate action plans in terms of accuracy, thoroughness, effectiveness, group participation, and implementation.

Students self-evaluate their sense of increased empowerment.

DISABILITIES ARE NOT BARRIERS

I am only one, but still I am one. I cannot do everything, but still I can do something; I will not refuse to do the something I can do. — Helen Keller

Scenario

You're all set to go to college, and the perfect college has sent you an acceptance letter. A tennis scholarship makes the cost seem actually reasonable, and you even find a great third-floor apartment. Just before you leave for school, you get into a car accident. The doctor says you'll be wheelchair bound for a year. There goes the scholarship for awhile. Yet you don't want to delay school by a year, so you decide to start this fall anyway. You start to consider all the changes: how will you get around? Can you get to your apartment, or will you have to move? Then you think about a fellow student at your high school who is blind. All of a sudden, you have much more empathy for the disabled. What will you do?

In some countries, people with disabilities are not *allowed* to attend universities; fortunately, in the United States, to accommodate such challenges provisions are made, such as the recent Americans with Disabilities Act. Yet even with support, people with disabilities have to make concessions and compensations in order to accomplish their goals. And some people with disabilities are not even recognized; males are five times more likely to be diagnosed with learning disabilities (LD), although it is likely that many more girls have LD than is supposed.

Suppose you have a disability. What are your needs? How can they be met? Would your gender make a difference in how you are treated or how you deal with disabilities? What can you and others do to facilitate your dreams?

Content Skills

* information about disabilities
* mainstreaming techniques
* teaching techniques
* interpersonal skills

Information Skills

* location skills
* determining main ideas
* transforming information into workshop form

Rationale for the Activity

About one-seventh of the U. S. population has some kind of disability. While society has become more aware and accepting of their presence, many people are still uncomfortable around such individuals. This activity helps students better understand disabilities and how both genders live with them. It also facilitates a pro-active approach to helping all people fulfill their potential.

Structure

Grade Level: middle and high school
Time Frame: 5-7 periods
Approach: working towards inclusiveness
Resources: resources about disabilities
Groupings: Arrange small heterogeneous groups by type of disability.

Activities

(1) In a large group discussion students share their observations about people with disabilities. Warm-up questions can include:
Have you been around people with disabilities? Describe your experiences.

Do you personally know anyone with disabilities? Describe your relationship with them.

Are you more comfortable with certain kinds of disabilities? Why?

How do you respond to people with disabilities?

How do you think that a person's gender affects how s/he deals with a
disability?

How do you think you would cope if you had a disability?

What measures do you know about that help people with disabilities?

One student records statements made by boys; one student records girls'
comments. Students discuss where they derive their ideas.

(2) (Optional) If time permits, students can experience disabilities through
    simulations, such as:
      • being blinded for a day
      • being wheel-chair bound for a day
      • having the dominant hand — or both hands — constrained in a bandage
    or mitten
      • wearing ear plugs for a day

At the end of the day, students comment on their experiences and how
they compensated for any constraints.

Note: Some disabilities such as learning disabilities are more difficult to
simulate, and may be harder for students to understand.

(3) The class then lists aspects of disabilities to research. Typical points
    include: disability characteristics, academic needs, physical needs, social
    needs, psychological needs, gender issues, relevant agencies, regulations,
    ways to help. The class is divided into small heterogeneous working
    groups. Each small group researches information about a specific dis-
    ability using the guiding list of aspects to organize data.

(4) Groups share their findings and determine what patterns emerge among
    disabilities.

(5) In a large group discussion students brainstorm ways to make people
    aware of issues connected with disabilities. Each small group develops a
    workshop about the disability researched.

Community Outreach

Students gather information from the community about disability
issues. They can conduct interviews, observe in agencies serving people with
disabilities, and examine accounts in local mass media. Students may brainstorm a list of feasible local experts, such as:

- individuals with disabilities
- groups dealing with disabilities
- health experts and settings

Culminating Experience

Groups meet with experts in the field of disabilities, and share their workshop plans.

Groups can conduct these workshops for other students or community groups.

Evaluation

Groups cross-evaluate lists and workshops in terms of accuracy, thoroughness, and presentation quality.

Local experts and persons with disabilities evaluate the workshops in terms of accuracy, thoroughness, appropriateness, and presentation quality.

EQUITY IN EDUCATION

Only the educated are free. — Epictetus

The mind is not sex-typed. — Margaret Mead

The highest result of education is tolerance. — Helen Keller

Scenario

Since you were a little kid you wanted to be a doctor. You take the standard college-prep courses and do well. You find out during the last semester, though, that you should have taken four years of mathematics. Your guidance counselor suggests that you go into nursing instead, especially since the medical field is so competitive. You begin to wonder how hard it will be to get the college preparation you need. Would you have a better chance entering your field in another country because of gender balance? How do you feel? What should you do?

How does gender factor in education? What is the gender mix in different college majors? What about your teacher models: do they follow a gender pattern as the education level rises? And what about today: are school courses, resources, and activities gender equitable? Does education mirror gender equity?

Content Skills

- knowledge about education courses
- career information
- legal knowledge

Information Skills

- location skills
- content analysis skills
- transforming information into chart form

Rationale for the Activity

Education should serve as a model of gender equity, yet the reality sometimes reveals another picture. What students experience in the way of models, and what opportunities they are given, largely determine the education they receive and the career choices they will make. This activity enables students to heighten their awareness of educational practices, and either compensate for inequalities or find ways to improve gender equity within education.

Structure

Grade Level: high school
Time Frame: 5-8 periods
Approach: focus on gender differential
Resources: resources on education, textbooks, legal sources on education, school and college catalogs. A good source is:
> Klein, Susan. *Handbook for Achieving Sex Equity through Education.* Baltimore: Johns Hopkins University Press, 1989.

Grouping: Arrange small heterogeneous groups by major.

Activities

(1) Large-group warm-up questions (on newsprint or other large surface one student records boys' statements; another student records girls' statements):

What are your favorite courses? Why?
What are your least favorite courses? Why?
What career plans do you have? Why?
Do you prefer male or female teachers? Why?
Do you think one gender or another makes for a better administrator? Why?
Do you think girls and boys get equal treatment in classes? Why?
What effect do you think gender has in education? Why?
The class analyzes the two lists of statements to discover possible patterns.

(2) The class lists factors for choosing a course or interest. From the discussion should arise issues of role-models, teaching techniques, personal preferences/personality, enjoyment of content, peer involvement.

(3) The large group then discusses how gender issues could be involved or affected. For example, are both genders equally represented and encouraged in all courses? Do school co-curricular activities treat genders equitably? (A good example is athletics.) How does school staffing reflect gender role-modeling?

(4) The class focuses on school textbooks, and generates a list of factors to look for when determining the degree to which a textbook treats gender issues equitably. Representative points include:
• **content:** relative status of genders, amount of content for each gender, variety of roles for each gender, positive and negative connotations for each gender, separate coverage of genders, amount of stereotyping
• **visuals:** relative to each gender represented and their mixture), setting of each gender (especially with regard to family life), status of each gender, roles of each gender, ages of people represented
• **references:** number of authorities cited per gender — if determinable

(5) The class is divided into small heterogeneous working groups. Each group analyzes textbooks in a different discipline, preferably in personal areas of interest. The groups report their findings, and the class discusses the conclusions.

(6) Pursuing the same discipline, small groups research the academic preparation (e.g., majors, degrees) needed to prepare for associated careers. They research the number of students in the major/degree program (surveying a number of colleges as is feasible, including abroad). They should also look at the number of females and males in their specified career

fields as well as the faculty gender representation. Groups present their findings to the large group by producing and interpreting graphs generated from their findings.

(7) One representative from each group makes up the second grouping. Those groups are arranged by college, and write comparisons on gender figures across curricular areas.

Community Outreach

Students can gather educational information from the community through interviews, visits, and institutional publications. Students may brainstorm a list of feasible local experts, such as college and high school counselors and faculty.

Culminating Experience

The class as a whole generates a written plan for improving gender equity in school environments. This may include: new courses such as women's studies, greater awareness and incorporation of gender issues in existing courses, enrichment of co-curricular opportunities for females, or other options. Each group may focus on one aspect of the plan. The plan can be presented to site, district, or regional administrators.

Evaluation

Groups cross-evaluate the graphs in terms of their accuracy, thoroughness, and appearance.

The class plan is evaluated in terms of its thoroughness, rationale, and justification by the teacher and associated administrators.

JOULES ARE
A GIRL'S BEST FRIEND

Energy is the power that drives every human being. It is not lost by exertion but maintained by it, for it is a faculty of the psyche. — Germaine Greer

Scenario

What gets you up in the morning? How do you deal with three o'clock slumps? What foods energize you — or make you look bloated? What about your own energy plant: your body? What fuels it? What *is* energy anyway, and what's the best source of power for human consumption and use?

Content Skills

- physics knowledge
- mathematics skills
- physiology knowledge

Information Skills

- location skills
- charting and interpreting data
- making comparisons
- determining correlations and cause-effect relations

Rationale for the Activity

Knowing how energy works helps explain the consequences of decisions concerning energy use. This activity examines the students' own energy sources and uses. The concepts of limited supplies of energy and alternative energy sources help students make more enlightened decisions about their use of energy. Particularly since girls sometimes exhibit a reluctance to pursue science topics, the practical nature of energy also facilitates student growth in physics and mathematics skills.

Structure

Grade Level: high school
Time Frame: 5-6 periods
Approach: working towards inclusiveness
Resources: resources on physiology, physics, energy, mathematics, statistics, graphing; materials for graphing (particularly computer applications); physiology measurement tools (optional). Good books include:

Brody, Jane. *Jane Brody's Nutrition Book.* New York: Bantam Books, 1987.
Fenn, John B. *Engines, Energy, and Entropy.* New York: W. H. Freeman, 1987.
Gartrell, Jack E. and Larry E. Schafer. *Evidence of Energy.* Arlington, VA: National Science Teachers Association, 1990.
Howes, Ruth and Anthony Fainberg, eds. *The Energy Sourcebook.* New York: American Institute of Physics, 1991.

Romer, Robert H. *Energy: An Introduction to Physics.* New York: W. H. Freeman, 1976.

Grouping: Arrange small heterogeneous groups by type of energy source or use.

Activities

(1) The class is divided into two groups: girls and boys. Within each group discussion, students define energy, then identify energy sources and uses. The two groups come together, and formal definitions of energy are provided. The class compares their definitions and sources/uses.

(2) Students then focus on their own energy plant: the human body. Students review what fuels the body, how food is converted into energy, and how the body then uses up energy.

(3) The class is divided into small heterogeneous working groups. Each small group researches the energy properties of a nutrient, e.g., carbohydrates, proteins, fats. Data are charted into the following categories (or other class-generated categories):
   • food sources and their caloric values
   • how food breaks down into energy
   • time it takes for food to convert into energy
   • type of energy generated/body reaction
   • possible gender differences in food/energy processing.

(4) One small group researches the amount of energy per hour expended for different kinds of activities, such as sleeping, swimming, eating.

(5) One representative from each group constitutes a new group, who choose a different type of person to chart energy and nutrient intake and expenditures. Each gender at different ages should be represented, including a pregnant woman. Each group mathematically charts that person's energy consumption and use during a day.

(6) Groups exchange charts and compare energy flows.

Community Outreach

Students gather information from the community about energy sources and uses. They can conduct interviews, observe companies and agencies, and examine local mass media reports. Students may brainstorm a list of feasible local experts, such as:

- scientists
- health experts: physicians, nutritionists, physical therapists
- medical/health settings
- recreational settings
- energy plants

Culminating Experience

Each group poses an energy situation, such as: mid-morning slump, overweight body, bulimia, pre-game preparation, late-night studying. Teams diagnose the energy flow (needs and use), and prescribe an energy-based solution. A panel of energy/nutrition experts rates the prescriptions.

Evaluation

Groups cross-evaluate charts for accuracy, thoroughness, and presentation quality.

Groups and experts cross-evaluate solutions for feasibility and scientific accuracy.

Groups self-evaluate their members' participation and peer teaching.

RELATING TO THE ENVIRONMENT

The maltreatment of the natural world and its impoverishment leads to the impoverishment of the human soul.
— Raisa Gorbachev

Scenario

It feels overwhelming at times. You hear about it every day: diminishing rainforests, dying species, thinning ozone. You see it all around you: litter, dirty water, smog. How did this happen? What can you do about it? Is this any way to treat Mother Nature?

Content Skills

- definition and description of environments
- activities that pollute the environment

- activities that improve the environment
- planning skills

Information Skills

- location skills
- determining main facts
- determining correlations and cause-effect relationships
- organizing and synthesizing information

Rationale for the Activity

Women are seeing the environment as a personal challenge and opportunity. Female-related activities such as fashion and home economics have harmed the environment. Females, such as Rachel Carson, have also paved the way to improve the environment. This activity raises student consciousness about the environment, causes of pollution — and ways to counteract it.

Structure

Grade Level: middle and high school
Time Frame: 7-10 periods
Approach: working toward inclusiveness
Resources: sources on the environment, biographies, environmental organizations. Good sources include:

> Diamond and Ornstein, eds. *Reweaving the World: The Emergence of Ecofeminism.* San Francisco: Sierra Books, 1990.
> Earth Works Group. *Environmental Actions: Simple Things Women Are Doing to Save the Earth.* Berkeley, CA: Earth Works Press, 1992.

Grouping: Arrange small heterogeneous groups by country, environmental issue, or industry.

Activities

(1) The class discusses what is meant by the environment; their perspectives should include the workplace as well as the wilds. In small groups students share their feelings about environmental issues. As each group reports generate a class list of issues. When done, the class can rank the relative importance of the issues and discover whether gender perspectives differ significantly.

(2) The class brainstorms ways that industry pollutes the environment, especially in terms of women-related industries such as cosmetics and

furs. They next brainstorm daily practices that pollute the environment (e.g., use of diapers, napkins, containers).

(3) Each group researches people and practices that pollute and improve the environment. The class decides how to assign groups: by country, industry, or environmental issue. Based on their findings, groups develop a "balance sheet" about their aspect of the issue. Note any gender issues; for example, in some countries women cannot be political decisionmakers. Each group reports their findings, and the class discusses the implications.

(4) After researching background information, each group focuses on one effort to improve the environment, traces the process, and ferrets out the obstacles and the ways they were overcome. Again, note if gender issues apply. Each group reports its findings, and the class discusses the implications.

Community Outreach

- governmental agencies
- community environmental organizations
- local businesses
- youth groups such as Scouts and 4-H

Culminating Experience

Triads formed from like interests design a practical plan that would result in helping the environment, taking into account the goal and the means. Triads can work with an existing agency or cause, or change one school-related practice with relation to the environment. For example: students can produce a videotape about local environmental issues, develop a database directory of local environmental resources and projects, or start an environmental campaign.

Environmentalists (particularly women) visit the class and share their experiences in planning and implementing ways to improve the environment. They can also review and critique student environmental plans.

Evaluation

Groups cross-evaluate group efforts to research their topic and create a balance sheet, examining accuracy and thoroughness.

At the second stage, groups cross-evaluate ability to analyze and develop plans to improve the environment.

CHICK, BROAD, GIRL, LADY, WOM*N

*When she stopped conforming to the conventional picture of
femininity she finally began to enjoy being a woman.*
— Betty Naomi Friedan

Scenario

It gets really confusing these days. Ads show older women in baby doll
dresses, movies show tough female newspaper executives, albums show
females in chains, Madonna shows all. There are Wonderbras and pinstripe
pants. What does it mean to look feminine, and how is that different from
being a female?

Content Skills

- perceptions about females and femininity
- psychology and sociology
- folklore
- communication

Information Skills

- content analysis skills
- determining correlations and cause-effect relationships
- visual literacy
- organizing and synthesizing information
- transforming information into a visual medium

Rationale for the Activity

The concept of femininity is much subtler than the biological reality
of being female. Cultural depictions and expectations of femininity change,
and those social norms influence female *and* male roles and actions. This
activity raises student awareness about social definitions of femininity, particularly through visual imagery: their origins, their manifestations, and
their influence. In the final analysis, each person defines femininity — and
masculinity.

Structure

Grade Level: middle and high school
Time Frame: 6-8 periods
Approach: focus on gender differential
Resources: visual sources (print and non-print resources on fashion, media, history), folklore books, periodicals. Good sources include:

> Brownmiller, Susan. *Femininity.* New York: Ballantine, 1984.
> *Confessions of the Guerrilla Girls.* San Francisco: HarperCollins, 1995.
> Dalby, Liza. *Geisha.* Berkeley, CA: University of California Press, 1983.
> Dayles, Susan J. *Where the Girls Are: Growing Up Female with the Mass Media.* New York: Random House, 1995.

Grouping: Arrange small heterogeneous groups by visual medium, culture, or historical period.

Activities

(1) Four large squares of newsprint are posted around the room, one for each of the following terms: feminine, masculine, female, male. Students go around the room writing words associated with each term. They should note their own gender beside each word they write.

(2) In a large-group discussion students analyze the characteristics generated for each cell above. Dictionary definitions are given for the four terms, followed by student reactions to the definitions. Discuss where students derive their ideas, and the extent to which they are influenced by these definitions.

(3) The large group discusses the following warm-up questions:
   What images do the media use to describe femininity?
   What images do the media use to describe masculinity?
   How important do you think it is to be feminine or masculine?
Then they brainstorm visual resources and discuss how to analyze visual images of femininity: body language, clothing and make-up, hair styles, action, setting, special relationships with other people. Using a couple of examples, the class develops a standard list of criteria for evaluating the image. Note that femininity is often defined in contemporaneous writing, including folklore.

(4) The class is divided into small heterogeneous working groups. Each group locates images of femininity for one historical period and critically analyzes the content and underlying message. Whenever possible,

groups should provide a sketch/copy of the image with written comments pointing to the related details as well as a justification for identifying the image as feminine. Each group also determines the parameters of femininity for the time period (i.e., did one standard for femininity exist, how rigid were standards, who determined the standards?).

(5) Groups share their findings, and the class compares the images and sources of definition.

(6) New groups are formed, consisting of one representative from each of the original groups. The new groups define femininity as they would like it to be, and create accompanying images or descriptions.

Community Outreach

Students gather information from the community about femininity and masculinity. They can conduct interviews, observe community members, and examine the local media. Students may brainstorm a list of feasible local experts, such as:
- "buyers" for clothing stores
- advertising agencies
- media industry representatives
- women's groups
- psychologists and sociologists
- hair stylist and cosmeticians

Culminating Experience

Students create visual montages of femininity (e.g., historic, contemporary, ideal) to show at community gatherings.

Evaluation

Groups cross-evaluate group content analysis of visual images in terms of conclusions reached and their justification.

Groups cross-evaluate the definitions and images of femininity in terms of their congruence and rationale.

A SOUND MIND
IN A SOUND BODY

Health is not a condition of matter but of Mind.
— Mary Baker Eddy

Scenario

Becoming a teenager really separates the boys from the girls. For young women a whole new set of bodily concerns must be dealt with, things that young men don't have to worry about. The biggest is, of course, reproduction-related issues.

And there are those "secondary" factors such as body redistribution and chemical changes that affect everyone's mental outlook. What health issues need to be addressed now?

Content Skills

- nutritional issues
- exercise issues
- female development

Information Skills

- location skills
- determining main facts
- determining correlations and cause-effect relationships
- recognizing patterns from data
- transforming information into chart form

Rationale for the Activity

Teenage females have two sets of health issues to deal with: adolescent growth and women's biological systems. Changes are more drastic for developing females than for males, and self-esteem often takes a nosedive as these changes occur.

In addition, the health field is still largely male-dominated, making it even harder for young women to come to terms with their changing bodies. This activity provides information about women's health issues and ways that young women can take charge of their own bodies.

Structure

Grade Level: middle and high school (treatment will differ according to age and sophistication)

Time Frame: 5-8 periods

Approach: focus on gender differential

Resources: resources on physical and psychological health and fitness, biology, substance abuse. Good sources include:

> Boston Women's Health Book Collective. *The New Our Bodies, Ourselves.* New York: Simon & Schuster, 1992.
>
> Golub, Sharon. *Health Care of the Female Adolescent.* New York: Haworth Press, 1984.
>
> Gray, Mary Jane, et al. *The Woman's Guide to Good Health.* Yonkers: Consumer Reports Books, 1991.
>
> Healy, Bernardine. *A New Prescription for Women's Health: Getting the Best Medical Care in a Man's World.* New York: Viking, 1995.
>
> Koblinsky, M., ed. *The Health of Women: A Global Perspective.* Boulder: Westview Press, 1993.
>
> McCoy, Kathy and Charles Wibbelsman. *The New Teenage Body Book.* New York: Putnam, 1992.
>
> *The PDR Family Guide to Women's Health and Prescription Drugs.* Montvale, NJ: Medical Economics Data, 1994.
>
> Shangold, Mona and Gabe Mirkin. *The Complete Sports Medicine Book for Women.* Rev. ed. New York: Simon & Schuster, 1992.
>
> Shephard, Bruce and Carroll Shephard. *The Complete Guide to Women's Health.* 2d rev. ed. New York: Penguin, 1990.
>
> Smyke, Patricia. *Women and Health.* London: Zed Books, 1993.

Grouping: Arrange small heterogeneous groups by health issues. Teachers should consider the needs of their students when discussing and researching topics. In some cases, single-sex groups or discussion sessions allow for more open discussion. The wishes of students should be honored as much as possible.

Activities

(1) Begin discussion of teen health issues by having same-sex pairs list myths and "truisms" about growing up and other health issues (e.g., "You can't get pregnant during your period" or "Chocolate makes you get acne" or "Only gays get AIDS"), making an index card for each statement. Then have pairs match up with pairs of the opposite sex to share their lists and brainstorm others. Index cards are gathered, and the teacher shares some with the class. Students can number a blank sheet, and write "True" or "False" as the statements are read (and numbered by the teacher). Students should expect to differ in their answers. The generated list starts

the group discussion about health issues, and provides research topics for testing their validity.

Another approach is to develop a set of health-related questions, such as: "Can you get a disease by having oral sex?" and "Do people go into heat like dogs?"

(2) The class discusses where they get information about health issues. If time permits, students can generate a list of sources and rank them according to frequency used and degree of credibility.

(3) The class is divided into small heterogeneous working groups optimally composed of two females and two males. Each group researches the female and male aspects of a specific health issue, such as: nutrition, exercise, body dimensions, reproductive changes, secondary sex changes. Each group creates a comparison chart to present their findings visually. Another way to divide groups is by body system (e.g., skeletel, digestive, etc.).

(4) The groups share their charts and determine what patterns may arise.

Community Outreach

Students gather information about health issues from the community through interviews, visits and observations, agency publications, and local mass media. Students may brainstorm a list of feasible local experts, such as:
- medical experts and settings
- athletic personnel
- family planning experts and settings
- legal experts

Culminating Experience

The class develops a game show based on their original myths and their research findings. They can present it to other classes, younger students, or youth groups. Game questions and answers should be reviewed by health professionals first.

Students develop a personal health plan based on the class findings.

Evaluation

Groups cross-evaluate group charts in terms of accuracy, thoroughness, and appearance.

The class game show is evaluated in terms of its accuracy and effectiveness of presentation.

Student health plans are evaluated in terms of their thoroughness and knowledge.

A HOME IS MORE THAN A ZIP CODE

The ideal of happiness has always taken material form in the house, whether cottage or castle; it stands for permanence and separation from the world. — Simone de Beauvoir

Scenario

Out on your own! No one to tell you to pick up your room. No one to tell you what to eat. You can design the place the way you want. So where will you live? How will you decide where to live? What do you need to know to get started in your own home?

Setting up your own place is an exciting adventure! It also entails lots of details and hidden costs. You may find that gender issues arise as well. It's not as easy as it sounds, so being prepared will help you when you know it's time to strike out on your own.

Content Skills

- housing factors
- budgeting
- comparative buying

Information Skills

- location skills
- interpreting information
- interviewing skills
- transforming data into chart form

Rationale for the Activity

Independent living involves numerous skills and factual knowledge. This activity helps students discover the different factors that enter into decisionmaking about a livable shelter, and facilitates their locating viable sources of information.

Structure

Grade Level: high school
Time Frame: 5-7 periods
Approach: working towards inclusiveness
Resources: newspapers, resources on insurance and banking, local sources about utilities
Grouping: Arrange small heterogeneous groups by topic.

Activities

(1) The class discusses the factors to consider when setting up independent living arrangements. Topics should include:
  • shelter or type of housing (rent vs. buy, choosing a place, utilities, furnishings, physical needs, size, maintenance, roommates, down payments)
  • settings (climate, geography, proximity to work or other needs)
  • food (nutrition, comparison-buying)
  • transportation (public vs. private, insurance and other expenses)
  • fiscal issues (bank accounts, credit cards, taxes)
  • insurance and other expenses.
A good way to begin the activity is to have students interview their parents/ guardians or other adult about the steps in setting up living arrangements.

(2) The class discusses possible gender issues such as roommates and different treatment by banks/landlords.

(3) The class is divided into small heterogeneous working groups. Each group researches the process and associated costs for one housing issue, and reports their findings to the rest of the class. Students should be encouraged to interview banks, housing services, insurance companies, or young adults in independent living situations.

Community Outreach

Students gather local housing information through interviews, visits, and local media. Students may brainstorm a list of feasible experts, such as:
  • housing services: landlords, etc.
  • banks and other financial institutions

- insurance companies
- students who live independently

Culminating Experience

Each small group is given a budget (e.g., $1000 a month) to plan their independent living arrangement. They should limit their housing needs to 40% of the budget. (The class should brainstorm other anticipated expenses, such as clothing or entertainment, an alternative culminating experience being a monthly budget of total financial responsibilities.) All figures and sites should be based on real data derived from newspapers, agencies, etc.

Evaluation

Groups cross-evaluate topical research in terms of thoroughness and accuracy.

At the second stage, groups cross-evaluate budgets in terms of realistic expectations and thoroughness.

LANDING A JOB

Skilled labor teaches something not to be found in books or in colleges. —Harriet Robinson

Scenario

You are ready to enter the Real World of Work. You want this first job to count as a stepping-stone to a real career so in most cases you don't want to spend time packing grocery bags. How do you know what to do? How do you land that dream job, or at least a job that counts?

Content Skills

- career information
- self-assessment skills
- interviewing skills

Information Skills

- location skills
- weighing factors
- translating information into game format

Rationale for the Activity

Most young people, female and male, can expect to work for pay at least twenty years, principally because they have to support themselves and other family members. Work also helps one's self-esteem and contributes to society. Each job experience shapes future career decisions, so time should be spent making thoughtful decisions about personal preferences and abilities. While the women's movement and related laws have helped equalize career opportunities, young women should be aware of possible barriers or obstacles to career ladders or equitable treatment as they make decisions that affect their futures.

Structure

Grade Level: high school
Time Frame: 7-10 periods
Approach: focus on gender differential
Resources: Career and self-assessment sources. Good sources include:
  Bloomberg, Gerri and Margaret Holden. *The Women's Job Search Handbook.* Indianapolis: Williamson, 1991.
  Harragan, Betty Lehan. *Games Mother Never Taught You.* New York: Warner, 1977.
  Iglitzin, Lynne B. *Focus on Careers.* Santa Barbara, CA: ABC-CLIO, 1991.
Grouping: Arrange small heterogenous groups by career or interest.

Activities

(1) The class takes a values inventory to discover personal priorities [handout at end]. Small groups discuss their inventories, and relate them to their career plans. Each group reports out a couple of significant findings.

(2) The class brainstorms factors in choosing a job. Points should include: abilities, time, commute, setting, education, gender, race, life style, transferability to long-term career, salary, friends or connections, language, family demands.

(3) The class brainstorms ways to get a job. Points should include: agencies, advertisements, friends, bulletin boards, personal networks, volunteer work.

(4) Students locate possible jobs and research/write appropriate resumes.

(5) Students hold mock interviews for desired jobs.

(6) Small groups research careers in terms of preparation, opportunities, barriers, and gender issues. Each group reports out their findings to the rest of the class.

Community Outreach

Students can gather information form the community about jobs. They can conduct interviews, read agency reports, and examine mass media. Students may brainstorm a list of feasible local experts, such as:
- employment agencies and headhunters
- local chambers of commerce
- local business women

Culminating Experience

Students hold a career fair, which is organized by a class steering committee made up of one representative from each small group.

Students create a career game, which includes job factors. For example, issues should include health, pregnancy, re-entry, disabilities, sexual orientation, national economy, etc., and their consequences.

Evaluation

Groups cross-evaluate career findings for accuracy and thoroughness.

The class game or career fair is evaluated in terms of its representation of issues, accuracy, and presentation.

Self-assessment Inventory

DIRECTIONS: Complete the following sentences honestly.

1. By the time I am 25 I will:
2. Three ways I like to spend my free time are:

3. Five skills I now have include:
4. I would like to be better at these four things:
5. My educational goal is:
6. My career goal is:
7. If I had 10 points, I would assign the following numbers to these job factors according to my interest and ability: numbers, people, things, ideas.
8. If I had 10 points, I would assign the following numbers to career, family, friends, self:
9. Sketch what you and your family will look like when you are 35 years old:
10. Write your obituary:

TAKE ME TO YOUR LEADER

You take people far as they will go, not as far as you would like them to go. — Jeannette Rankin

Scenario

Suppose there's an injustice that you want to rectify. Perhaps you want to push a cause. To make a difference you probably need to enlist the help of others, and that requires leadership. What does it take to be a leader? Are leaders born or made? How can you become a leader?

Content Skills

- leadership skills
- interpersonal skills
- knowledge about organizational behavior

Information Skills

- determining main ideas
- determining correlational and cause-effect relationships
- recognizing patterns from data
- transforming information onto a timeline

Rationale for the Activity

Young people want to make a difference. They also need to learn that usually they can be more effective if they work with others towards achieving a goal. This activity helps students identify leadership characteristics and develop leadership skills.

Structure

Grade Level: high school
Time Frame: 7-10 periods
Approach: focus on gender differential
Resources: leaders; leadership, organization and program development sources; biographies (especially autobiographies). Good overviews include:

Cantor and Burnay. *Women in Power — The Secrets of Leadership.* Boston: Houghton Mifflin, 1992.

Helgesen, S. *The Female Advantage: Women's Ways of Leadership.* New York: Doubleday, 1990.

Karnes, Frances and Suzanne Bean. *Girls and Young Women Leading the Way.* Minneapolis: Free Spirit Press, 1993.

Maher, Robert. *Leadership: Self School Community.* Reston, VA: National Association of Secondary School Principals, 1988.

Grouping: Arrange small heterogeneous groups by plan.

Activities

(1) In a guided vision experience students think about a leader whom they admire. They envision what that person looks like, what gestures and expression s/he uses, what s/he says and how it is said, how s/he acts, what s/he does, her/his setting. Afterwards, the class generate lists of leadership qualities, along the categories listed above. They then create a definition of a leader, and compare it to a dictionary definition. As lists are reviewed, students should examine the impact of gender on those qualities.

(2) In a large group discussion students list possible influential factors for leadership success, such as: sources of power, life experiences, personal background, personality, mentors, decision-making processes, public image, gender issues. As a follow-up, students link possible leadership factors to successful causes such as the Women's Liberation Movement, civil rights, United Farm Workers, Rainbow Coalition, and the Moral Majority.

(3) Each student chooses a leader and researches him/her in terms of the factors generated by the class. At least half of the leaders should be women. Students should be encouraged to read autobiographies and to interview local leaders. Each student creates a timeline, noting significant points in the leader's life. The line should be two-dimensional, with a curving line representing the relative highs and lows of the person's life. [*Note:* for easier comparison, one inch should represent 10 years.] Alternatively, the timeline can trace the "life" of one cause that the leader is known for.

(4) Students compare their charts and timelines in small groups, and determine what patterns emerge from the factors. Groups share their predictive factors for leadership, focusing on how factors relate to the success of a cause. Students should also examine how gender affects leadership or causes.

Community Outreach

Students gather information about leadership from the community through interviews, agency publications, and local mass media. Students may brainstorm a list of feasible local experts, such as:
- community service and business groups and their leaders
- award-giving groups
- cause groups

Culminating Experience

Small groups choose a cause to lead, and create a plan of action. Community leaders can evaluate these plans and provide guidance to students.

Alternatively, the class can design and implement a leadership workshop or course for schools or youth groups. Recognized community leaders can evaluate the course.

Evaluation

Groups cross-evaluate timelines and leader charts in terms of accuracy, thoroughness, and presentation quality.

Groups cross-evaluate predictive factors in terms of feasibility and justification of conclusions.

The leadership workshop is evaluated in terms of appropriateness, relevancy, group participation, leadership, and degree of success.

THERE OUGHT TO BE A LAW

Law and equity are two things which God hath joined, but which men hath put asunder. —C. C. Colton

Scenario

"Students have rights!" "Everyone is equal in the sight of the law!" Are those statements true? Do women, in particular, get different treatment — either preferential or second-rate — because of their gender? What is the law, and how can you help make it more gender equitable?

Content Skills

- legal issues
- planning and writing skills

Information Skills

- location skills
- determining main facts
- interpreting and organizing skills

Rationale for the Activity

The Equal Rights Amendment did not pass for a variety of reasons. This activity enables students to examine current gender-related legal issues, and facilitate ways to advance gender equity in light of the law.

Structure

Grade Level: high school
Time Frame: 4-6 periods
Approach: focus on gender differential
Resources: legal resources. A couple of good sources on sexual harassment are:

> Morrison, Celia. *Bearing Witness: Sexual Harassment and Beyond — Everywoman's Story.* Boston: Little, Brown and Company, 1994.

Strauss, Susan. *Sexual Harassment and Teens.* Minneapolis: Free Spirit, 1992.

Grouping: Arrange small heterogeneous groups by legal issue.

Activities

(1) Large-group warm-up questions (one or two students take group notes for everyone to see):

Do you think men and women are treated equally under the law? Why?

What laws do you know of that focus on women's rights?

Do you think that women need special laws? Would that be discrimination?

What are some gender-sensitive issues that might call for legislation?

(2) The class discusses how gender issues are treated under the law. They may already be acquainted with the Equal Rights Amendment, the Nineteenth Amendment, and Title IX, and should brainstorm other gender-related laws or possible areas of legislation (e.g., day care, maternity care, other health issues, education, employment, sexual activity, violence). Both attitudes and prior knowledge about gender-related legal issues should surface.

(3) The class brainstorms aspects of researching legal issues. Points to consider should include: social context, history of the law, implications, challenges to the law, impact of the law.

(4) The class is divided into small heterogeneous working groups. Each group researches one specific gender-related law or one legal issue, covering its different aspects. Each group shares its findings by acting as legal "experts," whom the rest of the class interrogate about the law. Alternatively, each group creates a hypermedia presentation on the legal issue.

Community Outreach

Students gather legal information from the community through interviews, observing law creation or enforcement, reading local legislation, or examining local legal action. Students may brainstorm a list of feasible local experts, such as:

- legal experts
- law libraries
- local business people and other groups affected by gender-related laws

- law enforcement officers
- school administrators

Culminating Experience

The class develops a hypermedia "expert system" about gender-related issues by linking the various group hypermedia files. (This can be done by a small editing committee of students.)

Alternatively, students can craft a piece of legislation to present to a law-making body.

Evaluation

Groups cross-evaluate student subject experts and expert systems in terms of their accuracy, thoroughness, and presentation.

Legal experts can evaluate the expert system in terms of its accuracy, thoroughness, and presentation. They can also evaluate the piece of legislation in terms of its legality, feasibility, and wording.

MEASURING UP

Men have always detested women's gossip because they suspect the truth; their measurements are being taken and compared.
— Erica Jong

Scenario

You look at the models in the magazines, and feel that you can't measure up to them. It's embarrassing in gym because you don't look normal-sized. Then someone tells you they weigh 85 kilos, and you don't know whether that's anorexic or overweight. What is normal? What's in the healthy range? Is there an ideal?

Content Skills

- measurement and conversion skills
- physiological knowledge

Information Skills

- location skills
- reading and interpreting numerical data
- classifying and transforming data into graphs and tables

Rationale for the Activity

Students "size" each other and themselves frequently. They also come into contact with different measurement units. This activity gives students the opportunity to make meaningful applications of measurement skills, and to explore the issues of "normalcy" in terms of body dimensions.

Structure

Grade Level: high school
Time Frame: 4-6 periods
Approach: working towards inclusiveness
Resources: conversion tables, resources on body measurements (particularly in the areas of fitness and nutrition), clothing resources (fashion, sewing). A couple of good sources include:

> Brumberg, Joan Jacobs. *Fasting Girls: The History of Anorexia Nervosa.* New York: New American Library, 1989.

> Chernin, Kim. *The Hungry Self: Women, Eating & Identity.* New York: Times Books, 1985.

Grouping: Arrange small heterogeneous groups by age, type of measurement, or period in history.

Activities

(1) Large-group warm-up questions (for everyone to see, one student records girls' statements and one student records boys' statements):

What do you think are the ideal measurements for boys and girls your age?

What is your basis for determining ideal body measurements?

Do you feel comfortable with your body measurements?

How important do you think body measurements are?

All students write down their best guess ideal measurement for their age and gender. The class examines their impressions, and compares boys' and girls' answers. Then they discuss where they get their ideas about ideal measurements.

(2) The teacher or student finds current health charts on desirable body measurements, and shares them with the class. The basis for the medical figures is also shared.

(3) The class brainstorms measurements related to the body: vital statistics, nutrition, fitness. They then brainstorm factors that change measurements: age, health, culture, history. The class covers descriptive statistical concepts: mean, median, range, normal distribution and variance.

(4) The class is divided into small heterogeneous working groups. Each group researches one type of measurement, finding numerical data for each gender, different age groups, and historical period (if possible). Each group produces comparison bar graphs to present their findings visually.

(5) The same groups convert their measurements into another unit of measure (i.e., inches into centimeters), and produce a conversion table of their data.

(6) The class discusses the findings and decides if "ideal" exists.

(7) Each student finds his/her measurements with respect to age and gender, then with respect to another age or gender. They then write up their findings.

Community Outreach

Students gather information about body measurements form the community through interviews, observations, and local publications. Students may brainstorm a list of feasible local experts, such as:
- medical experts and settings
- athletic experts and settings
- fitness experts and settings

Culminating Experience

The class surveys themselves or another population in terms of body measurements, and produces a series of graphs showing normal distribution of the sample population and its relationship to standard measurements.

Evaluation

Groups cross-evaluate graphs and tables in terms of their numeric accuracy and appearance.

IT'S A SMALL WORLD

*The more I traveled the more I realized that fear makes
strangers of people who should be friends.*
— Shirley MacLaine

*If we are to achieve a richer culture, rich in contrasting val-
ues, we must recognize the whole gamut of human poten-
tialities, and so weave a less arbitrary social fabric, one in
which each diverse human gift will find a fitting place.*
— Margaret Mead

Scenario

An increasing number of foreign-born students are entering your
school. You see them around, and feel somewhat uncomfortable as they talk
in a language you can't understand. They don't dress as you do either, and
they sometimes seem to stare at you. One night you hear your parents talking about their places of work. Your father says that the union won't let in
any non-citizens. Your mother is concerned because some of the foreign-
born mothers are bringing their children into work, and it's affecting the
office. You know that many people are escaping oppression in their native
country, and others want a better living, but you begin to wonder if maybe
your education is going to be brought down because of these outsiders.
What should you do?

There's a saying that the flutter of a butterfly can be felt around the
world; that is, each one's actions affects others. An earthquake in Japan affects
the U. S. stockmarket. Student violence in one school causes other schools
to question their own safety and security measures. A nun's work in a Third
World country impresses people worldwide. What makes the world tick?
How are we all alike and different? How can we work together for good?

On a more personal level, what are the chances that you will travel to a
foreign country, or that you will meet someone from outside the United
States? Immigration is a big issue. Why do people come to this country? How
do they affect others in the U. S.? How does the confrontation of the two
cultures affect women in particular? How can you deal with the situation?

Content Skills

• knowledge about immigration: legalities, economics, education, language, acculturation, gender
• interpersonal skills

Information Skills

- location skills
- distinguishing fact from opinion
- identifying biases and patterns
- determining correlations and cause-effect relations
- identifying patterns and trends
- interviewing skills
- transforming information into chart form

Rationale for the Activity

The United States is a land of immigrants. Within the country, almost 14% of the population principally speak a non-English language, an increase of 38% over the last ten years. About a million people legally immigrate to the States; illegal entrances swell the numbers. In fact, California has no majority ethnic group; everyone is a minority. This sizable population significantly affects the United States, both positively and negatively, depending on one's perspective.

This activity helps students become more critically aware of immigration issues, and their roles in relationship to these people. Frankly, the hope is that students will appreciate the richness of diversity, and work positively for the inclusion of all people into American society.

Structure

Grade Level: middle and high school
Time Frame: 6-8 periods
Approach: working towards inclusiveness
Resources: resources on immigration, materials for producing games. A couple of good sources include:

>Davis, Angela Y. *Women, Race & Class.* New York: Random House, 1983.
>Featherstone, Elena. *Skin Deep: Women Writing on Color, Culture, and Identity.* Freedom, CA: Crossing Press, 1994.

Grouping: Arrange small heterogeneous groups first by immigration issue, then into game groups.

Activities

(1) In a large-group discussion students share their knowledge and feelings about people from different countries, then about immigrants to the United States. The class compares impressions between these two categories of

people, and discusses the reasons for differences and the sources of those opinions.

(2) In small heterogeneous groups, students brainstorm about how immigration affects the United States, listing factors of influence. After sharing their findings with the whole class, each group chooses one factor to research. Issues will typically include: economics, language, socialization, laws and regulations, education, culture and customs, religion and beliefs.

(3) Each group locates information about their factor. Students should be encouraged to contact local immigration agencies and recent new Americans, including fellow students. To guide their data gathering, groups can chart their findings into a grid:

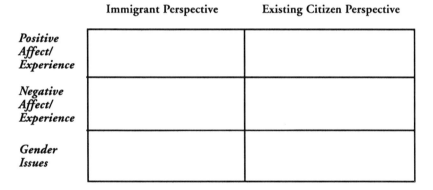

	Immigrant Perspective	Existing Citizen Perspective
Positive Affect/ Experience		
Negative Affect/ Experience		
Gender Issues		

(4) New groups are formed, one per grid "cell," with representation from each of the original groups. The new groups look for patterns and discrepancies in the findings, and share their interpretations with the entire class.

Community Outreach

Students gather information about immigrants by interviewing and observing within the community and reading local accounts. Students may brainstorm a list of feasible local experts, such as:
- immigration agencies
- immigrants and their social groups, such as religious and fraternal institutions
- social service agencies
- local chambers of commerce

Culminating Experience

The class develops a plan of action for new immigrants within their school or other local group. The plan should include ways to help immigrants and existing citizens deal positively with the factors researched earlier. Ideas might include referral information, sensitization workshops, welcome kits, buddy programs, and brochures/illustrated guides. Local representatives can review and incorporate the plans.

Evaluation

Groups cross-evaluate the findings, both by factor and by grid "cell" in terms of accuracy, clarity, thoroughness, and justification of conclusions.

Plans of action are evaluated in terms of appropriateness, feasibility, accuracy of perception, presentation qualities, and potential impact.

MAKING BEAUTIFUL MUSIC TOGETHER

Music relates sound and time and so pictures the ultimate edges of human communications. — Iris Murdoch

Scenario

When you think of music, what comes to mind? Rock concerts? MTV? Graphic covers? What role do women play in the lyrics and in performing? How can music support and affirm women?

Content Skills

- music composition skills
- performance skills
- knowledge about musicians and the music industry
- knowledge about media industry

Information Skills

- location skills
- content analysis skills
- surveying skills

Rationale for the Activity

Music plays a significant role in society, and in the lives of teenagers in particular. Music also reflects social norms. This activity raises student consciousness about the image of women in music, and the participation of women in composing and performing music.

Structure

Grade Level: middle and high school
Time Frame: 6-8 periods
Approach: focus on gender differential
Resources: print and non-print resources on music (emphasis on visual and audio sources), including compositions, the music industry, and musicians. An excellent source of women's songs is:

> Wenner, Hilda and Elizabeth Freilicher. *Here's to the Women: 100 Songs for and about American Women.* Syracuse, NY: Syracuse University Press, 1987.

A new book that examines the music scene in terms of gender issues is:

> Reynolds, Simon and Joy Press. *The Sex Revolts: Gender, Rebellion, and Rock 'n' Roll.* Cambridge, MA: Harvard University Press, 1995.

Grouping: Arrange small heterogeneous groups by aspect of music or musical genre.

Activities

(1) In a large-group discussion students share their insights about contemporary music. Some guiding questions include:

What kind of music is popular among youth?

What influence does music have on youth?

What image do females have in music, such as in lyrics or visual representations? Why?

What role do females play in the composing and performance of music? Why?

How is music marketed?

What gender differences exist in music? Why?

Survey the class members' musical preferences, and interpret the results along gender lines.

(2) Next, the class identifies the steps in producing a record; they should include composition (lyrics and music), performance, production, marketing/selling. A small group may need to research this process and share it with the rest of the class.

(3) The class is divided into small heterogeneous working groups. Each group chooses one step in producing a record, and determines what tasks are involved. They should find out what gender issues exist, and survey the representation of males and females at each point. They then interpret the results, and pose ways to foster gender equity.

(4) As an alternative approach, each group can pick a decade or musical genre, and perform content analysis on representative lyrics in terms of gender image. Still another way to explore women's contributions to music is to study the lives of famous women composers and performers.

(5) Groups share their findings, and the class compares the gender representations.

(6) New groups are formed, consisting of one representative from each of the original groups. The new groups create a piece of music that is gender equitable in process and product.

Community Outreach

Students gather information about music within the community through interviews, concerts, and local mass media. Students may brainstorm a list of feasible local experts, such as:
- musical groups
- advertising agencies
- mass media sources (e.g., radio and TV stations, newspapers)

Culminating Experience

Each group performs their original piece of music. A student steering committee invites music industry representatives to share their experiences, highlighting gender issues.

Evaluation

Each group can cross-evaluate group content analysis of gender issues in terms of conclusions reached and their justification, as well as in terms of fostering gender equity.

Each group can cross-evaluate group original music in terms of quality and gender equity.

The steering committee is evaluated in terms of their ability to plan and implement a program about gender issues in music.

LET THERE BE PEACE ON EARTH

Courage is the price that life exacts for granting peace.
— Amelia Earhart

Scenario

What if there was a war and nobody came? When you read about the conflicts in other countries, when you hear about troubled homes, you wonder, "Can there be peace?" Is peace a passive state, or is it something that you really have to work at? Is peace a sex-linked trait? If peace starts with each one of us, then how can we generate peace within others?

Content Skills

- conflict resolution
- concepts of war and peace
- knowledge about psychology

Information Skills

- content analysis skills
- interviewing skills
- transforming information into visual and written forms

Rationale for the Activity

In an era of increasing violence and conflict, the voice of peace must be heard. Students need to see peace as an active choice, not a state of inaction. Especially as females are considered the peacemakers, this activity helps students visualize concepts of peace that can be applied actively by both sexes in daily life and in more global situations.

Structure

Grade Level: middle and high school
Time Frame: 4-6 periods
Approach: working towards inclusiveness
Resources: resources on peace and conflict resolution; art materials
Grouping: Arrange small heterogeneous groups by scenario.

Activities

(1) In a large-group discussion students define and describe the concepts and scenarios of peace and war. As a warm-up activity, students can write personal impressions about peace, using the following suggested prompts:

What is your definition of peace?

What was a time of peace for you? Describe it. What made it peaceful?

What are your hopes for peace?

Why do people want peace? Why do people want war?

What is the relationship, if any, between inner peace and peace among nations?

What gender connotations and issues are associated with war and peace? Why?

(2) The class is divided into small heterogeneous working groups. Each group selects one area of conflict; it may be in terms of relationships (e.g., divorce, teen-parent fights, etc.), local issues, national (e.g., abortion, capital punishment, etc.), or between nations. Each group researches the following aspects:

- description of the conflict
- reasons for the conflict
- consequences of the conflict
- possible solutions (and their consequences)
- gender issues, if any

(3) Each group researches an existing peace plan and determines how successful the plan has been. Using the plan as a model, each group poses a peace plan for the area of conflict researched and justifies its stance.

(4) Groups share their findings and discover possible commonalities.

Community Outreach

Students gather information about peace efforts within the community. They can conduct interviews, examine legal documents, and read local accounts of peace-making efforts. Students may brainstorm feasible experts in the field, such as:

- arbitrators
- government officials
- advocacy groups, especially of women

Culminating Experience

The class holds a peace summit. Each group poses their reasons and plans for peace. Students can be encouraged to create original works that express peace: art, music, poetry. This summit can be videotaped for public community broadcasting, or covered by the local press.

Evaluation

Groups cross-evaluate peace plans for the viability and thoroughness of solutions, consequences, and justification.

Groups self-evaluate how effectively they worked together in terms of participation, shared leadership, successful negotiations, and respectful communication.

RAISING CAIN AND CANDY

If you bungle raising your children, I don't think whatever else you do well matters very much.
— Jacqueline Kennedy Onassis

Scenario

One of your classmates is pregnant, and she's going to have the baby. She gets lots of attention, and everyone is sweet to her. She has it all worked out: she can get a GED degree, her mother will take care of the baby during the day so she can work, her boyfriend says he'll marry her once he gets some money, and in a couple of years she can go to college. And she'll have a sweet little bundle of joy to hug and kiss and call her own. Maybe getting pregnant isn't so bad, even though to this point you've been pretty careful about any sexual activity.

Babies are so cute and so dependent. Motherhood is considered a prime blessing in life. Fathering a child is a macho thing. These are some of the truisms surrounding parenthood. But they don't talk about the hidden costs and sacrifices associated with raising a child. Nor are the gender inequalities about sons and daughters spoken openly. Is now the time to have a child? Is there a right time? What factors will result in the most advantageous upbringing?

Content Skills

- child-rearing practices
- health issues
- economic issues

Information Skills

- location issues
- determining main facts
- determining correlations and cause-effect relationships
- interviewing skills
- transforming information into a chart or skit format

Rationale for the Activity

A surprising number of young women have children, often out of wedlock, as a means to bolster self-esteem and nurture another human being. This activity shows students the overt and covert costs of raising a child, and emphasizes the female role that society foists on these mothers.

The goal is that young people will make reasonable decisions about having and raising children.

Structure

Grade Level: high school
Time Frame: 4-6 periods
Approach: focus on gender differential
Resources: child-rearing sources. Some good sources include:

Beyer, Kay. *Coping with Teen Parenting.* New York: Rosen, 1995.

Cassell, Carol and Pamela M. Wilson. *Sexuality Education: A Resource Book.* New York: Garland, 1989.

Eagle, Carol J. and Carol Colman. *All That She Can Be.* New York: Simon & Schuster, 1993.

Lindsay, Jeanne. *Teen Dads: Rights, Responsibilities, and Joys.* Buena Park, CA: Morning Glory Press, 1993.

Masland, Robert P., Jr. and David Estridge, eds. *What Teenagers Want to Know about Sex: Questions and Answers.* Boston: Little, Brown, 1988.

Michael, Robert T. *Sex in America: A Definitive Survey.* Boston: Little, Brown and Company, 1994.

Pittman, Karen Johnson. *Adolescent Pregnancy: Whose Problem Is It?* Washington, DC: Children's Defense Fund, 1986.

Pittman, Karen Johnson and Gina Adams. *What About the Boys? Teenage*

Pregnancy Prevention Strategies. Washington, DC: Children's Defense Fund, 1988.

Simpson, Carol. *Coping with Teenage Motherhood.* New York: Rosen, 1992.

Grouping: Arrange small heterogeneous groups by factors/issues.

Activities

(1) In small groups students share their recollections of early childhood. Some guiding questions are:

What made them happy?

What were their stresses?

How would they raise their own children differently or the same?

What gender issues arose? Why?

Groups share some of their insights with the rest of the class.

(2) The class discusses why people want children. Then they brainstorm the needs of children, and the costs (e.g., financial, time, and psychological) associated with those needs. Issues raised should include: prenatal care, housing, clothing, food, safety, medical and health needs, insurance, care/supervision. Gender issues of responsibility and medical needs should be emphasized.

(3) Each group researches the varied costs (financial, time, psychological) associated with each issue. They report their findings in terms of a chart or skit to the rest of the class. Groups should be encouraged to interview community experts and experienced friends. (An alternative approach is to research changing attitudes and responsibilities of child-rearing over time.)

Community Outreach

Students gather community information about having children. They can conduct interviews, observe child-adult interactions, and examine local media coverage. Students may brainstorm a list of feasible subject experts, such as:

- day-care experts and settings
- parents
- medical experts and settings

Culminating Experience

The class produces a series of skits about child-raising for peers, younger students, or community members.

Evaluation

Groups cross-evaluate the findings in terms of credibility and thoroughness.

Skits are evaluated in terms of their credibility and coverage.

GETTING TO KNOW YOU

Let the world know you as you are, not as you think you should be, because sooner or later, if you are posing, you will forget the pose, and then where are you? — Fanny Brice

Scenario

You've met the most awesome person, but you're afraid that you aren't the Right Someone. You try to get some inside dope on the person: personal interests, usual haunts, the social crowd, preferences in food and clothing, aspirations. Now if you can match all those items, you'll be set! Or will you? Your dreamboat hands you a joint, and you know your parents would flip out if they found out. But you're also afraid that the relationship will stop before it even has a chance to begin. What should you do?

Think about all the people who affect you: your family, your friends, other peers and adults. In what do they influence your decisions now? How will they determine your future? How do you want relationships to affect your life?

Content Skills

• psychology and sociology knowledge
• decision-making skills

Information Skills

• location skills
• determining correlations and cause-effect relationships
• interviewing skills
• transforming information into skit format and timelines

Rationale for the Activity

Teenagers often make decisions based on their relationships with people. They may follow or rebel against other peoples' opinions. This activity facilitates student awareness of relationships and their potential impact on personal decisionmaking.

Structure

Grade Level: middle and high school
Time Frame: 4-6 periods
Approach: working towards inclusiveness
Resources: psychology and sociology resources. Good sources include:
  Poe, Elizabeth A. *Focus on Relationships.* Santa Barbara, CA: ABC-CLIO, 1993.
  Scarf, J. *Intimate Partners.* New York: Ballantine, 1987.
  Walters, M. *The Invisible Web: Gender Patterns in Family Relationships.* New York: Guilford Press, 1988.
Grouping: Arrange small heterogeneous groups by type of relationship.

Activities

(1) The class discusses relationships in teen lives: peers (boys and girls), parents, other family, other adults, cultural groups, community. The class determines whether boys and girls differ in their attitudes. Some warmup questions include:
  Who are the most important persons in your life right now? Why?
  In what areas of your life do you make decisions?
  What influence do other people have on your decisions?
  Who has the most influence on your decisionmaking right now? Why?
  Who would you like to be the most important person in your life? Why?
  Students may rank their types of relationships in terms of their importance (now and ideal).

(2) Students do self-surveys to determine to what extent these relationships affect their lives and their decisionmaking by drawing a family timeline to record significant events and decisions. The line should include the decision and the person(s) who influenced the decision. Students then share their decision timelines in small heterogeneous groups, and report any patterns to the class.

(3) The class is divided into small heterogeneous working groups. Each group researches one type of personal relationship, comparing it in terms

of historical and cultural contexts. Each group shares its findings in the form of a skit to the rest of the class.

(4) One representative from each group constitutes a new group, each of which researches one relationship event: dating, marriage, parenting, divorce, and death. Each person brings a unique perspective to the event. Each group shares its findings in the form of a skit to the rest of the class.

Community Outreach

Students gather information about relationships within the community. They can conduct interviews, make visits and observations, and examine local media coverage. Students may brainstorm a list of feasible experts in the field, such as:
  • counselors
  • parents

Culminating Experience

Each small group develops a scenario about relationship issues, such as peer pressure or dating practices. The class discusses the issues raised and applies them to different relationships and individual responses to them. The skits and follow-up discussions can be presented to younger students or peer classes.

Evaluation

Groups cross-evaluate skits in terms of their accuracy, thoroughness, and believability.

The class is evaluated in terms of its discussion and rationale for individual stances.

WHICH GENDER IS GOD?

There is a God within us. — Ovid

God is a verb, not a noun. — Richard Buckminster Fuller

Scenario

In visiting a museum you see a sculpture of the Goddess Mother. What is your image of God? Is God created in the image of man? Some say that men classify women as Madonnas or Magdalenas, perfect or sinful; is this fair or accurate? Where do women fit into the spiritual realm?

Content Skills

- women's and men's roles in religions
- mythology

Information Skills

- location skills
- determining main facts
- identifying patterns from a variety of data
- distinguishing between fact and opinion
- determining correlations and cause-effect relationships
- transforming information into different forms

Rationale for the Activity

Feminist and ecologically sensitive religions are making a comeback as women explore avenues that more closely satisfy their spiritual needs. This activity enables students to study the historical and social context of religion as it treats gender issues, and helps students explore their own spiritual choices.

Structure

Grade Level: high school
Time Frame: 5-7 periods
Approach: focus on gender differential
Resources: resources on religion, spiritualism, sociology, psychology, and women's issues. Good sources include:

> Anderson, Sherry Ruth and Patricia Hopkins. *The Feminine Face of God: The Unfolding of the Sacred in Women.* New York: Bantam, 1992.
>
> Berger, P. *The Goddess Observed: From Goddess to Saint.* Boston: Beacon Press, 1988.
>
> Bolen, Jean Shinoda. *Goddesses in Everywoman.* New York: Harper & Row, 1984.

Chernin, Kim. *Reinventing Eve: Modern Woman in Search of Herself.* New York: Time Books, 1987.

Eisler, Riane. *The Chalice and the Blade.* San Francisco: Harper & Row, 1987.

Heine, Susanne. *Matriarchs, Goddesses, and Images of God.* Minneapolis: Augsburg, 1989.

Radl, Shirley Rogers. *The Invisible Woman: Target of the Religious New Right.* New York, Dell, 1983.

Rutter, Virginia Beane. *Woman Changing Woman: Feminist Psychology Re-conceived Through Myth and Experience.* San Francisco: HarperCollins, 1993.

Shussler, Fiorenza. *In Memory of Her: A Feminist Theological Reconstruction of Christian Origin.* New York: Crossroads, 1992.

Stanton, Elizabeth. *The Original Feminist Attack on the Bible (The Woman's Bible).* New York: Arno Press, 1974.

Stone, Merlin. *When God Was a Woman.* New York: Harcourt Brace Jovanovich, 1978.

Walker, Barbara G. *The Women's Encyclopedia of Myths and Secrets.* San Francisco: Harper & Row, 1983.

Grouping: Arrange small heterogeneous groups by culture or religion.

Activities

(1) The class discusses the connotations of God: e.g., a grey-bearded distant man, an Earth mother goddess, an asexual scientific force field. They then discuss how those connotations arise.

(2) The class brainstorms ways to examine gender issues in religion/spiritualism: leadership roles, models to emulate, goddess figures, responsibilities and accountability of women, rites of passage, etc.

(3) The class is divided into small heterogeneous working groups. Using the class list of factors to examine, each group researches women spiritual models and women's roles in a specific culture or religion. Each group determines how to present its findings to the rest of the class: collage, skit, chart; a useful structure is to show the Ideal Woman/Goddess and the Representative Woman/Human. Another approach is by historical period, although this is harder to research.

(4) (Optional) Each group researches the characteristics of female figures in mythology. Following the mythic strand, the class discusses the characteristics of a mythical hero and heroine, and traces the hero/heroine quest.

Community Outreach

Students gather community information about religion and spirituality through interviews, visits, and religious documents. Students may brainstorm a list of feasible local experts, such as religious/spiritual leaders.

Culminating Experience

Each student designs a personal heroic quest/journey to become her/his own spiritual model. Students share their personal plans and experience in pairs.

Evaluation

Groups cross-evaluate research findings in terms of accuracy, thoroughness, and presentation quality.

Student quest/journey plans are evaluated in terms of mythic characteristics and personal engagement.

KEEPING SAFE AND SOUND

Only in growth, reform, and change, paradoxically enough,
is true security to be found. —Anne Morrow Lindbergh

Scenario

"A woman ought to be able to walk down the street naked with a $1000 bill pasted on her chest and not be harassed." Is that a social reality? Should it be? Despite the appearance of equal opportunity, women feel unequal when it comes to personal safety. For instance, the repercussions of rape if inflicted on a male cannot match those for a female. What scenarios exemplify issues that women must deal with? What can women do to insure personal safety? What measures can a woman take if she is not safe?

Content Skills

- knowledge about safety issues and measures
- knowledge about legal issues and measures

- self-defense skills
- knowledge about crime prevention

Information Skills

- location skills
- interviewing skills
- content analysis skills
- determining correlations and cause-effect relationships
- organizing and synthesizing information
- transforming information into simulation form

Rationale for the Activity

Young women have to look out for themselves. Families cannot protect them as much these days, both because parents are absent and because young women are in places independent of family much of the time. A young woman's opportunities are also greater: for good and for possible danger. This activity helps young women to analyze scenarios that could threaten personal safety and to develop means to avoid and deal with these situations.

Structure

Grade Level: middle and high school
Time Frame: 5-7 periods
Approach: focus on gender differential
Resources: resources on safety and simulations, "props" for simulations
Grouping: Arrange small heterogeneous groups by scenario.

Activities

(1) In a large-group discussion students describe potentially personally unsafe scenarios. In particular, they identify gender differences in terms of safety issues. Examples may include: baby-sitting, dating, traveling, being in a place alone.

(2) Taking one possible scenario, the class explores the following aspects:
   - description of the situation
   - factors that make the situation possibly unsafe
   - preventative measures
   - dealing with unsafe consequences (e.g., accidents)
   - relevant gender issues

(3) The large group brainstorms sources of information about personal safety measures. Besides print sources, students should be encouraged to seek information from community agencies. Students may need to practice interviewing skills.

(4) The class is divided into small heterogeneous working groups. Each group chooses a unique scenario and gathers facts about each aspect of it. Group representatives should contact community agencies to get documents and interview experts.

(5) Groups organize their findings by developing a simulation of the scenario. They may create several outcomes, depending on the gender of the persons involved and the manner in which persons in the situation react.

Community Outreach

Students gather community information about safety practices. They can conduct interviews, visit agencies, and examine their publications. Students may brainstorm a list of feasible local experts, such as:
- police
- hospitals and American Red Cross
- youth agencies: scouting, boys/girls clubs, religious groups, recreation centers
- legal groups
- women's groups

Culminating Experience

Each group performs a simulation of the hazardous scenario. In each case, the group should point out the preventative and coping skills needed. Community safety representatives can comment and expand on the information given. The simulations can be videotaped for use as training devices within the community.

Evaluation

Each group can cross-evaluate the simulations in terms of perceived accuracy and thoroughness, and in terms of presentation effectiveness.

The teacher and community representative can evaluate the simulations in terms of accuracy and thoroughness.

SCIENTIST LIFE LINES
— AND DATABASES

Science is voiceless; it is the scientists who talk.
— Simone Well

Scenario

As a kid you loved mixing ingredients and finding out what happened, especially baking soda and vinegar. You liked collecting rocks and shells, not just because they were pretty but because you wanted to know how they were formed. Your lab books are the most detailed in the class, and you find yourself wondering if you really have a chance of becoming a scientist. However, you don't see many women scientists around. On television, the serious scientists are men.

There's just one woman science teacher, and she teaches biology, which you don't like (cutting up frogs is not your idea of fun). She's also a middle-aged single woman, and you want to get married and have children. Can you really have it all?

Scientists are typically pictured as nerdy-looking men in white lab coats. What future is there for women in science? What kind of women tend to be scientists? What preparation is necessary to become a scientist? Do women have to face obstacles that men might not? Do they have to sacrifice a private life to become a scientist? Indeed, could women scientists bring a different perspective to science?

Content Skills

- classification skills
- transforming information into timelines
- knowledge about women scientists and their achievements
- hypothesis formation and testing

Information Skills

- location skills
- sequencing skills
- using databases
- transforming information into database form
- sorting skills

Rationale for the Activity

Science classes have used time lines to help students with sequencing skills. A geological era is one standard unit for timelines. Another typical science activity is classification, as in plant or animal identification. This lesson takes advantage of these two concepts and introduces the use of electronic databases as a means to facilitate sorting and sequencing of women scientists. Just as the scientific method can be used in experiments, the same use of hypothesis testing will be applied to analyzing women scientists.

This is a chance for students to see if women scientists have been centered in certain periods of history, areas of the world, or areas of study. They can use this information as they explore career options, especially in the hard sciences.

Structure

Grade level: middle and high school
Time Frame: 5 periods
Approach: focus on gender differential
Resources: computer database application program, resources about women scientists. A couple of reference sources include:

> Ogilvie, Marilyn Bailey. *Women in Science: Antiquity Through the Nineteenth Century; A Biographical Dictionary with Annotated Bibliography.* Cambridge, MA: MIT Press, 1986.
>
> Stanley, Autumn. *Mothers and Daughters of Invention.* Metuchen, NJ: Scarecrow Press, 1993.

Grouping: Arrange small heterogeneous groups by types of scientists.

Activities

(1) Large-group warm-up questions (one or two students take group notes for everyone to see):

What is your image of a scientist?

What are some characteristics that you associate with scientists?

Name some women scientists.

Do you think women are underrepresented in the field of science? Why?

(2) In a large-group discussion students share their perspectives and explain how they form their opinions. Then they form hypotheses about the lives of women scientists.

(3) The class discusses what kinds of information they want to include about each woman scientist: dates, nationality, field of study, family life,

etc. From those factors, they create a database "template," assigning one field to each kind of information.

(4) The class is divided into small heterogeneous working groups. Using the fields as a guide, each group researches a number of woman scientists (by scientific field, by country, or by historic era). If the template is designed at the start, each group can copy the form and just fill in the blanks with the information found when inputting the data onto the computer program. If the program allows one to merge several database files, each group can input on a separate computer or data disk. Otherwise, groups will have to take turns inputting.

(5) Each group develops a working hypothesis about the women scientists, such as: "Women scientists assigned are distributed equally across time" or "All fields of science are equally represented among the women scientists researched." (These statements are examples of *null hypotheses*.) They sort the resultant women scientists database by one or more fields, depending on their hypothesis.

If the data seem sequential, such as date of birth, the group places the data along a line.

If the data seem grouped, the group produces a graph of the data. *Note:* some integrated application programs allow you to transform the data directly into graph form.

By examining the line or graph, each group can determine whether their hypothesis was correct or not.

(6) Groups share their hypotheses and resultant representations of the data. They should determine what patterns, if any, exist across charts. Based on their findings, the class brainstorms ways to encourage more women to become scientists.

Community Outreach

Students gather information from the community about scientists, preferably women in the field. They can conduct interviews, visit sites, and read local accounts. Students may brainstorm a list of feasible local experts, such as:

- industries with science components
- medical and health facilities
- public agencies with science components

Culminating Experience

A student steering committee plans a panel discussion about women scientists, inviting educators and practitioners of both genders to talk about gender issues.

Alternatively, groups can produce videotapes about women scientists, which they can show to other students or the community at large.

Evaluation

Groups cross-evaluate databases in terms of the data's accuracy in reflecting each woman scientist's life and the analysis of the data justifying the group's conclusions.

The steering committee's efforts are evaluated in terms of their plan and its implementation.

Local experts and audiences evaluate student videotapes in terms of the content's accuracy and thoroughness, and on the quality of the presentation (e.g., organization, technical skill, effectiveness).

COVERING SPORTS

Sports can't help you win the game of life. Unless you get to play. — Women's Sports Foundation

Scenario

If you're on a girls' basketball team, what are the chances that you will be covered by the press, in comparison to boys' basketball? Are opportunities limited for women who want to participate in competitive sports? Is athletics a viable career for women? What can you do to change the picture?

Content Skills

- types of sports (male, female)
- types of media covering sports

Information Skills

- content analysis
- analyzing primary sources
- evaluating data for bias
- classifying data by developing a spreadsheet

Rationale for the Activity

While Title IX requires equal treatment of sports education in terms of gender, societal treatment of sports activity is not equitable. This activity enables students to see how gender influences sports participation and media coverage.

Structure

Grade Level: high school
Time Frame: 5-7 periods
Approach: focus on gender differential
Resources: different media: TV, newspapers, radio, magazines, yearbooks, literature. A couple of background resources include:

> Messner, Michael J. and Donald F. Sabo. *Sex, Violence, and Power in Sports.* Freedom, CA: Crossing Press, 1994.
> Nelson, M. B. *Are We Winning Yet? How Women Are Changing Sports and Sports Are Changing Women.* New York: Random House, 1991.

Grouping: This project may be grouped in two ways: by media or by sport. The most efficient method is by medium.

Activities

(1) The class generates a list of possible sports and sports-covering media. A class grid of sports vs. media (with separation between men's and women's sports) is constructed.

(2) The class discusses how to measure media coverage: by frequency, percentage of games covered, length of coverage, depth of coverage, placement in the publication, presence of accompanying photos, etc. Students should be sure to separate coverage by men from coverage by women, noting coverage of coed sports.

(3) The class is divided into small heterogeneous working groups. Each group tracks and evaluates one medium's coverage of all sports, being sure to separate coverage of men's sports from the women's counterpart.

(4) Each group completes its section of the class grid, and compares the medium's coverage of each sport, reporting their findings to the class.

(5) Groups should be re-assigned, one sport per group. They should analyze the grid data, comparing coverage of men and women in the particular sport. Their findings are shared with the class.

Community Outreach

Students gather local sports information through interviews, observations, and local media coverage. Students may brainstorm a list of feasible experts, such as:
- local recreation departments
- local media
- coaches and athletic directors

Culminating Experience

Women athletes and sports reporters lead a discussion about opportunities and limitations for women in sports. A representative from each group forms the steering committee to invite experts to the class and to plan the discussion.

Students write in local newspapers or report on local radio shows about women's sports.

Evaluation

Groups cross-evaluate group efforts in content analysis of media coverage.

At the second stage, groups cross-evaluate group content analysis of given data in terms of conclusions reached, and their justification.

The steering committee is evaluated in terms of their planning and implementation.

WORLDWIDE SUFFRAGE

Men, their rights and nothing more; women, their rights and nothing less. — Susan B. Anthony

Women who rock the cradle should rock the boat.
— Susan B. Anthony

Scenario

You are concerned about the welfare of your community and the ineffectiveness of the present political system. You also notice the underrepresentation of women in elected positions. You want to make a difference. What can you do?

Content Skills

- political knowledge
- legal knowledge, especially of voting rights
- historical knowledge of suffrage movement
- planning skills for political action

Informational Skills

- location skills
- interviewing skills
- using primary sources
- determining main facts
- determining cause-effect relationships
- determining trends

Rationale for the Activity

One of the most significant ways for women to gain power is through effective legislation and legislators. Generally, women are underrepresented in the political field. While women were "given" the vote with the 19th Amendment (1920), they have continued to fight for legal power. This activity enables students to explore the historical course of voting rights and to analyze feminism as a political movement.

Structure

Grade Level: high school
Time Frame: 8-10 periods
Approach: focus on gender differential
Resources: politicians, legal sources, books and non-print sources on politics and human rights
Grouping: Heterogeneous groups will examine different aspects of voting rights, either by country or by decade.

Activities

(1) Large-group warm-up questions (for all to see, one student writes down girls' statements and one student writes down boys' statements for follow-up comparison):

What words come to mind when I say "suffrage"?

Name some women in politics.

Do you think men and women are equally represented in politics?

Do you think it would be a good idea to have political representation be proportional to the number of each gender? Why?

How would you feel about having a female President? Why?

Students discuss the basis for their political views.

(2) Suffrage is formally defined: as the right to vote — and to exercise that right. Students discuss definition.

(3) The class brainstorms the various aspects of suffrage. Points that should arise include:
   • history of suffrage movements
   • political roles of men and women in different countries
   • comparison of legal rights and practices

(4) The class is divided into small heterogeneous working groups. Each group determines which aspect of suffrage to research and which points to consider in each case. Issues should include:
   • male vs. female rights and practices
   • social and political patterns of the times
   • causes for political status and change
   • organizations and individuals who effected change

(5) Groups report their findings, and develop a written plan to increase female political power.

Community Outreach

Students gather community information about politics. They can conduct interviews, participate in political events, and examine local media coverage. Students may brainstorm a list of feasible political experts, such as:
   • local politicians
   • League of Women Voters
   • school board members

Culminating Experience

Local women politicians hold a panel discussion about their career paths in politics. Alternatively, the League of Women Voters can share their experiences about politics and women's issues. A student steering committee plans the panel discussion and local arrangements.

Students help in political campaigns and report their experiences.

Evaluation

Groups cross-evaluate their research efforts in terms of sources, legal issues found, and political plans based on information.

The steering committee is evaluated in terms of their planning and implementation.

Bibliography

HUMAN DEVELOPMENT

Brooks-Gunn, Jeanne and Anne C. Petersen, eds. *Girls at Puberty: Biological and Psychological Perspectives*. New York: Plenum, 1983.

Brown, Lyn Mikel-Brown and Carol Gilligan. *Meeting at the Crossroads: Women's Psychology and Girls' Development*. Cambridge, MA: Harvard University Press, 1992.

Debold, Elizabeth, Marie Wilson and Idelisse Malave. *Mother Daughter Revolution: From Good Girls to Great Women*. New York: Bantam, 1993.

Fausto-Sterling, Anne. *Myths of Gender: Biological Theories about Women and Men*. New York: Basic Books, 1992.

Gersoni-Stavun, D. *Sexism and Youth*. New York: Xerox, 1974.

Orenstein, Peggy. *School-girls*. New York: Doubleday, 1994.

Pipher, Mary. *Reviving Ophelia: Saving the Selves of Adolescent Girls*. New York: Putnam, 1994.

EDUCATION

Bateson, Mary Catherine. *Composing a Life*. New York: Atlantic Monthly Press, 1989.

Berne, Patricia H. and Louis M. Savary. *Building Self-Esteem in Children*. New York: Continuum, 1990.

Blakey, Elaine and Sheila Spence. "Developing Metacognition." *ERIC Digest*. (Nov. 1990): 1-2.

Brooks, Jacqueline Grennon and Martin G. Brooks. *In Search for Understanding: The Case for Constructivist Classrooms*. Alexandria, VA: Association for Supervision and Curriculum Development, 1993.

Cane, Renate Nummela and Geoffrey Caine. *Making Connections: Teaching and The Human Brain*. Alexandria, VA: Association for Supervision and Curriculum Development, 1991.

Center for Early Adolescence. School of Medicine. The University of North Carolina at Chapel Hill. *Living with 10- to 15-Year-Olds: A Parent Education Curriculum*. Revised ed. Chapel Hill, NC: University of North Carolina, 1992.

Derman-Sparks, L. and ABC Task Force. *Anti-Bias Curriculum: Tools for Empowering Young Children*. Washington, D.C.: National Association for the Education of Young Children, 1989.

Eagle, Carol J. and Carol Colman. *All That She Can Be*. New York: Simon & Schuster, 1993.

Eisenberg, Michael B. *School Library Media Programs: Thriving in the Technological Jungle*. Miami Beach: American Library Association, 1994.

Equal Rights: An Intergroup Education Curriculum. Harrisburg: Pennsylvania Department of Education, 1976.

Estes, Sally, ed. *Growing Up Is Hard to Do*. Chicago: American Library Association, 1994.

Farmer, Lesley S. J. *Cooperative Learning Activities in the Library Media Center*. Englewood, CO: Libraries Unlimited, 1991.

_____. *Leadership Within the School Library and Beyond*. Worthington, OH: Linworth Publishing, 1995.

Gilligan, Carol. *In a Different Voice*. Cambridge, MA: Harvard University Press, 1982.

Gray, Mattie Evans. *Images: A Workbook for Enhancing Self-Esteem and Promoting Career Preparation, Especially for Black Girls*. Sacramento: California Department of Education, 1988.

Hannigan, Jane Anne and Hilary Crew. "A Feminist Paradigm for Library and Information Science." *Wilson Library Bulletin* (October 1993): 28-32.

Harding, Sandra. *Whose Science? Whose Knowledge?: Thinking from Women's Lives*. Ithaca, NY: Cornell University Press, 1991.

Henes, Robby. *Creating Gender Equity in Your Teaching*. Davis, CA: University of California, 1994.

Hotchkiss, Carol W. *Quests & Quandaries: A Human Development Workbook*. Washington, DC: Avocus, 1993.

How Schools Shortchange Girls. Washington, DC: American Association of University Women and the National Education Association, 1992.

Howe, Florence, ed. *High School Feminist Studies*. Old Westbury, NY: Feminist Press, 1976.

Jackson, Bailey W. and Evangelina Holvino. "Organizational States of Multicultural Awareness." Unpublished paper, 1981.

Jackson, Stevi. *Women's Studies: Essential Readings*. New York: New York University Press, 1993.

Jipson, Janice. *Repositioning Feminism and Education: Perspectives on Educating for Social Change*. Westport, CT: Greenwood Press, 1995.

Kamarck Minnich, Elizabeth. *Transforming Knowledge*. Philadelphia: Temple University Press, 1990.

Klein, Susan S., ed. *Handbook for Achieving Sex Equity through Education*. Baltimore: Johns Hopkins University Press, 1984.

Krimmelbein, Cindy Jeffrey. *The Choice to Change*. Englewood, CO: Libraries Unlimited, 1989.

Layman, Nancy. *Sexual Harassment in American Secondary Schools*. Dallas: Contemporary Research, 1994.

Listening for All Voices: Gender Balancing the School Curriculum. Summit, NJ: Oak Knoll School of the Holy Child, n.d.

Messick, S. *Individuality in Learning*. San Francisco: Jossey-Bass, 1976.

Middleton, Sue. *Educating Feminists: Life History and Pedagogy*. New York: Teachers College Press, 1992.

Promoting Self-Esteem in Young Women: A Manual for Teachers. Albany: New York State Education Department, n.d.

Reiff, Judith C. *Learning Styles*. Washington, DC: National Education Association, 1992.

Roiphe, Katherine. *The Morning After: Sex, Fear, and Feminism on Campus*. Boston: Little, Brown, 1994.

Sadker, Myra and David Sadker. *Failing at Fairness: How America's Schools Cheat Girls.* New York: Charles Scribner's Sons, 1994.

———. *Sex Equity Handbook for Schools.* New York: Longman, 1982.

Sanders, Jo and Mary McGinnis. *The Computer Equity Set.* Metuchen, NJ: Scarecrow Press, 1991.

Schmitz, Betty. *Integrating Women's Studies into the Curriculum: A Guide & Bibliography.* New York: Feminist Press, 1985.

Spanier, Bonnie, ed. *Toward a Balanced Curriculum: A Sourcebook for Initiating Gender Integration Projects.* Cambridge, MA: Schenkman, 1984.

Stafford, Beth, ed. *Directory of Women's Studies Programs & Library Resources.* Phoenix: Oryx Press, 1990.

Tschudi, Stephen. *Young Learner's Handbook.* New York: Macmillan, 1987.

Vandergrift, Kay. "A Feminist Research Agenda in Youth Literature." *Wilson Library Bulletin* (October 1993): 23-27.

Vocational Education Journal. March 1993; sex equity issue.

Williams, Constance. "Does Different Equal Less? A High School Woman Speaks Out." *School Library Journal* (January 1973): 36-38.

PSYCHOLOGY

Armstrong, Thomas. *7 Kinds of Smart.* New York: Penguin Books, 1993.

Belenky, Mary Field, et al. *Women's Ways of Knowing.* New York: Basic Books, 1986.

Bolen, Jean Schinoda. *Goddesses in Everywoman.* New York: Harper & Row, 1984.

Cameron, Julia. *The Artist's Way.* New York: Putnam, 1992.

Eisler, Riane. *The Chalice and the Blade.* San Francisco: Harper & Row, 1987.

Haraday, Keith and Eileen Donahue. *Who Do You Think You Are?* San Francisco: Harper Collins, 1994.

Heine, Susanne. *Matriarchs, Goddesses, and Images of God.* Minneapolis: Augsburg, 1989.

James, Muriel and Dorothy Jongeward. *Born to Win.* New York: New American Library, 1971.

Johnson, Robert. *She: Understanding Feminine Psychology.* New York: Harper & Row, 1977.

Koberg, Don and Jim Bagnall. *Values Tech.* Los Altos, CA: William Kaufmann, 1976.

Lerner, Gerda. *The Creation of Feminist Consciousness.* New York: Oxford University Press, 1994.

McFarland, Rhoda. *Coping Through Self-Esteem.* Revised ed. New York: Rosen, 1993.

Macoby, E. and C. Jacklin. *The Psychology of Sex Differences.* Stanford: Stanford University Press, 1974.

Mikel-Brown, Lyn and Carol Gilligan. *Meeting at the Crossroads: Women's Psychology and Girls' Development.* New York: Charles Scribner's Sons, 1994.

Miller, Jean Baker. *Toward a New Psychology of Women.* Boston: Beacon Press, 1976.

Moir, Anne and David Jessel. *Brain Sex.* New York: Dell, 1991.

Murdock, Maureen. *The Heroine's Journey.* Boston: Shambhala, 1990.

Noble, Kathleen. *The Sound of a Silver Horn: Reclaiming the Heroism in Contemporary Women's History.* New York: Fawcett, 1994.

Sanford, Linda T. and Mary Ellen Donovan. *Women and Self-Esteem; Understanding and Improving the Way We Think and Feel About Ourselves.* New York: Penguin, 1985.

Tannen, Deborah. *You Just Don't Understand*. New York: William Morrow, 1990.
Unger, R. and M. Crawford. *Woman and Gender: A Feminist Psychology*. New York: McGraw-Hill, 1992.

SOCIAL ISSUES

Aburdene, Patricia and John Naisbitt. *Megatrends for Women*. New York: Random House, 1992.
Allgeier, Elizabeth R. and Naomi B. McCormick, ed. *Changing Boundaries: Gender Roles and Sexual Behavior*. Palo Alto: Mayfield Publishing, 1983.
Barber, Elizabeth. *Women's Work: The First 20,000 Years*. New York: W. W. Norton, 1994.
Benatovish, Beth, ed. *What We Know So Far: Wisdom Among Women*. New York: St. Martin's Press, 1995.
Chesler, Phyllis. *Patriarchy*. Monroe, ME: Common Courage Press, 1994.
Degler, Carl N. *At Odds: Women and the Family in America: From the Revolution to the Present*. New York: Oxford University Press, 1980.
Denfeld, Pene. *The New Victorians: A Young Woman's Challenge to the Old Feminist Order*. New York: Warner Books, 1995.
Faludi, Susan. *Backlash: The Undeclared War Against American Women*. New York: Crown, 1991.
Featherstone, Elena. *Skin Deep: Women Writing on Color, Culture, and Identity*. Freedom, CA: Crossing Press, 1994.
Findlen, Barbara. *Listen Up: Voices from the Next Feminist Generation*. Seattle: Seal Press, 1995.
"Fourth World Conference on Women." *UN Chronicle* (June 1995): 39–48.
French, Marilyn. *The War Against Women*. New York: Ballantine Books, 1992.
Hamner, Trudy J. *Taking a Stand Against Sexism and Sex Discrimination*. New York: Franklin Watts, 1990.
Hirsch, Marianne and Evelyn Fox Meller, eds. *Conflicts in Feminism*. New York: Routledge, 1990.
Hoy, Pat C. *Women's Voices: Voices and Perspectives*. New York: Random House, 1989.
Lunardini, Christine A. *Women's Rights*. Phoenix: Oryx Press, 1994.
Mann, Judy. *The Difference: Growing Up Female in America*. New York: Warner, 1995.
Martin, Renee and Don Martin. *The Survival Guide for Women*. Washington, DC: Regnery Gateway, 1991.
Miller, Neil. *Out of the Past: Gay and Lesbian History from 1869 to the Present*. New York: Random House, 1995.
Namjoshi, Suniti. *Feminist Fables*. North Melbourne, Australia: Spinifex, 1981.
Pollitt, Katha. *Reasonable Creations: Essays on Woman and Feminism*. New York: Knopf, 1994.
Rix, Sara E. *American Women 1990-91: A Status Report*. New York: Norton, 1990.
Rose, Phyllis, ed. *The Norton Book of Women's Lives*. New York: Norton, 1993.
Rosenberg, Rosalind. *Divided Lives; American Women in the Twentieth Century*. New York: Harper Collins, 1992.
Sapiro, V. *Women in American Society*. 2d ed. Mountain View, CA: Mayfield Publishing, 1990.
Schaef, Anne Wilson. *Women's Reality*. San Francisco: Harper & Row, 1985.

Stan, Adele M., ed. *Debating Sexual Correctness: Pornography, Sexual Harassment, Date Rape, and the Politics of Sexual Equality*. New York: Dell, 1995.

The Woman's Way. New York: Time-Life Books, 1995.

Wells, Diana, comp. *Getting There: The Movement Toward Gender Equity*. New York: Carroll and Graf, 1994.

Wolf, Naomi. *The Beauty Myth*. New York: Doubleday, 1992.

____. *Fire with Fire*. New York: Random House, 1994.

OUTSTANDING WOMEN

Bacon, Margaret Hope. *Mothers of Feminism*. Minneapolis: University of Minnesota Press, 1995.

Barchers, Suzanne I. *Wise Women: Folk and Fairy Tales from Around the World*. Englewood Cliffs, CO: Libraries Unlimited, 1990.

Bell-Scott, Patricia. *Life Notes: Personal Writings by Contemporary Black Women*. New York: W. W. Norton, 1994.

Council for Women in Independent Schools. *Many Women's Voices*. 2 vol. Washington, DC: National Association of Independent Schools, 1994.

Hine, Darlene Clark, ed. *Black Women in America*. Brooklyn: Carlson, 1994.

James, Edward and Janet James. *Notable American Women*. 3 v. Cambridge: Belknap, 1971.

Mervin, Sabrina. *Women Around the World and Through the Ages*. Wilmington, DE: Atomium Books, 1990.

Piland, Sherry. *Women Artists: An Historical, Contemporary and Feminist Bibliography*. 2nd ed. Metuchen, NJ: Scarecrow Press, 1994.

Reese, Lyn and Jean Wilkinson, eds. *Women in the World: Annotated History Resources for the Secondary Student*. Metuchen, NJ: Scarecrow Press, 1987.

Siegel Mary-Ellen. *Her Way: A Guide to Biographies of Women for Young People*. Chicago: American Library Association, 1984.

Stanley, Autumn. *Mothers and Daughters of Invention*. Metuchen, NJ: Scarecrow Press, 1993.

Who's Who of American Women. Chicago: Marquis, annual.

Williams, Ora. *American Black Women in the Arts and Social Sciences: A Bibliographic Survey*. 3rd ed. Metuchen, NJ: Scarecrow Press, 1994.

Woolum, Janet. *Outstanding Women Athletes*. Phoenix: Oryx Press, 1992.

World's Who's Who of Women. Cambridge, England: International Biographical Centre, biennial.

REFERENCE WORKS

Anderson, Bonnie S. and Judith P. Zinsser. *A History of Their Own: Women in Europe from Prehistory to the Present*. New York: Harper & Row, 1989.

Atkinson, Steven D. and Judith Hudson, eds. *Women Online: Research in Women's Studies Using Online Databases*. New York: Haworth Press, 1990.

Ballou, Patricia K. *Women: Bibliography of Bibliographies*. 2d ed. Boston: G. K. Hall, 1986.

Barrett, Jacqueline K., ed. *Encyclopedia of Women's Associations Worldwide*. Detroit: Gale Research, 1993.

Blain, Virginia, et al. *The Feminist Companion to Literature in English: Women Writers from the Middle Ages to the Present.* New Haven, CT: Yale University Press, 1990.

Brennan, Shawn. *Women's Information Directory.* Detroit: Gale Research, 1993.

Brennan, Shawn and Julie Winkle Pleck. *Resourceful Woman.* Detroit: Visible Ink, 1994.

Carter, Sarah and Maureen Ritchie. *Women's Studies: A Guide to Information Sources.* London: Mansell, 1990.

Dimona, Isa and Constance Herndon, eds. *The 1995 Information Please Women's Sourcebook.* Boston: Houghton Mifflin, 1994.

Franck, Irene and David Brownstone. *The Women's Desk Reference.* New York: Viking, 1993.

Hinding, Andrea, ed. *Women's History Sources: A Guide to Archives and Manuscript Collections in the United States.* 2 vol. New York: R. R. Bowker, 1980.

A History of Women in the West. 5 vol. Cambridge, MA: Harvard University Press, 1994.

Ireland, Norma Olin. *Index to Women of the World from Ancient to Modern Times: A Supplement.* Metuchen, NJ: Scarecrow Press, 1988.

Jorgensen, Mary Anne. *Directory of Selected Research and Policy Centers Working on Women's Issues.* 5th ed. Washington, DC: Women's Research and Education Institute, 1989.

McHenry, Robert, ed. *Her Heritage: A Biographical Encyclopedia of Famous American Women.* Cambridge, MA: Pilgrim New Media, 1995.

Maggio, Rosalie. *The Beacon Book of Quotations by Women.* Boston: Beacon Press, 1992.

_____. *The Dictionary of Bias-Free Usage.* Phoenix: Oryx Press, 1991.

Mumford, Lara Stempel. *Women's Issues: An Annotated Bibliography.* Metuchen, NJ: Scarecrow Press, 1989.

Ogilvie, Marilyn Bailey. *Women in Science: Antiquity Through the Nineteenth Century; A Biographical Dictionary with Annotated Bibliography.* Cambridge, MA: MIT Press, 1986.

Olsen, Kirstin. *Chronology of Women's History.* Westport, CT: Greenwood, 1994.

Reese, Lyn and Jean Wilkinson, eds. *Women in the World: Annotated History Resources for the Secondary Student.* Metuchen, NJ: Scarecrow Press, 1987.

Schneir, Miriam, ed. *Feminism in Our Time.* New York: Random House, 1994.

Seager, Joni and Ann Olson. *Women in the World: An International Atlas.* New York: Simon & Schuster, 1986.

Searing, Susan. *Introduction to Library Research in Women's Studies.* Boulder: Westview Press, 1985.

Statistical Record of Women Worldwide. 2nd ed. Detroit: Gale Research, 1995.

Taeuber, Cynthia, ed. *Statistical Handbook on Women in America.* Phoenix: Oryx Press, 1991.

Tierney, Helen, ed. *Women's Studies Encyclopedia.* 3 vol. Glenview, IL: Greenwood, 1989-91.

Trager, James. *The Women's Chronology: A Year-by-Year Record from Prehistory to the Present.* New York: Henry Holt, 1994.

Tuttle, Lisa. *Encyclopedia of Feminism.* New York: Facts on File, 1986. 399p. $24.95.

Uglow, Jennifer S., ed. *The Continuum Dictionary of Women's Biography.* Rev. ed. New York: Crossroad/Continuum, 1989.

Weiss, Daniel Evan. *The Great Divide; How Females and Males Really Differ.* New York: Poseidon, 1991.

Women's Action Coalition. *WAC Stats; The Facts About Women.* New York: New Press, 1994.

Women's Annual. Boston: G. K. Hall, annual.

GOOD SOURCES OF INFORMATION

American Association of University Women

Feminist Periodicals

Feminist Press

Films for the Humanities & Sciences: Women's Studies

International Network of Women in Technology (WITI@crl.com)

Internet

National Museum of Women in the Arts (Washington, DC)

National Women's History Project

Seeking Educational Equity and Diversity Project (SEED), Wellesley College Center for Research on Women

United States Department of Labor Women's Bureau

University of Maryland

Women's Educational Equity Act Publishing Center, Office of Educational Research and Improvement, U.S. Department of Education

Women's Studies Abstracts

Index